DEATH IN THE MOUNTAINS

Dear Sheila,
I do hope you enjoy this story — have a happy birthday!!
All the best,
Lisa
Florence 2008/9

DEATH IN THE MOUNTAINS

The True Story of a Tuscan Murder

LISA CLIFFORD

MACMILLAN
Pan Macmillan Australia

First published 2008 in Macmillan by Pan Macmillan Australia Pty Limited
1 Market Street, Sydney

Copyright © Lisa Clifford 2008

The moral right of the author has been asserted.

All rights reserved. No part of this book may be reproduced or transmitted by any person or entity (including Google, Amazon or similar organisations) in any form or by any means, electronic or mechanical, including photocopying, recording, scanning or by any information storage and retrieval system, without prior permission in writing from the publisher.

National Library of Australia
Cataloguing-in-Publication data:

Clifford, Lisa.
Death in the mountains: the true story of a Tuscan murder/author, Lisa Clifford.

ISBN: 9781405038683 (pbk.)

Bruni, Artemio.
Murder—Italy—Tuscany.
Tuscany (Italy)—Social life and customs.
Tuscany (Italy)—Rural conditions.

945.50929

Typeset in 12/16.5pt Stempel Garamond by Midland Typesetters, Australia
Printed in Australia by McPherson's Printing Group

Papers used by Pan Macmillan Australia Pty Ltd are natural, recyclable products made from wood grown in sustainable forests. The manufacturing processes conform to the environmental regulations of the country of origin.

Author photograph: James Cotier

Their lives were so very hard but, oh, the smiles on their faces as they recalled this, their lost way of life. Their eyes took on that faraway look, all misty and sentimental, as they remembered the Tuscany of their childhoods, the land of their grandfathers and grandmothers. These are their stories. That my imagination could ever be as rich as the truth in this book.

Foreword

This is the true story of the murder of Artemio Bruni, a peasant farmer in the mountains of Casentino, north-eastern Tuscany, in the winter of 1907. Artemio was my husband's great-grandfather.

Grandpa Artemio's death was never investigated. It was not reported to the police, nor did Bruna Bruni, Artemio's wife, ever demand justice. How could that be possible, I asked my mother-in-law – mafia? 'No, no, you don't understand,' she answered. 'Things were different in the mountains one hundred years ago. Grandpa and Grandma were poor farmers, no one could have cared less about them. Grandpa was a nobody and life was cheap in Tuscany then.'

In 1907 up to seventy per cent of rural Tuscany was farmed under the *mezzadria* farming system. Whole families worked as sharecroppers who paid half of everything they produced to their land's owners. Once the owners had been paid, the food left over for the *mezzadro* (farmer) was barely sufficient to avoid starvation.

One of the reasons I felt I had to write this book was to explain how incredibly hard life was for the rural Tuscan only one or two generations ago. There is enormous international focus on Tuscany and its glamorous villas, with little understanding of what actually went on inside them. These country houses are renovated and turned into luxury holiday destinations. But who did they belong to? How did the families who occupied them live and think? While writing, I discovered that the old traditions of country life are being lost, even in Italy itself.

Unable to resist my growing fascination with the old farming ways and the intrigue of an unexplained murder in the family, I felt compelled to find out more about Grandpa Artemio and Grandma Bruna. So on holiday visits to relatives in Casentino I started to talk to the old people about them. Strangely, the more questions I asked, the more murder scenarios came to light. Suddenly everyone had a theory on the long-ago slaying of Artemio Bruni. Cousins remembered what their grandfathers had said about the night he lost his life. Rickety old farmers, who had trouble remembering what had happened five minutes ago, recalled with great clarity what their uncles had said about the man from Casa sul Poggio. Each person I spoke to gave me an impression of the real characters described in these pages. From their accounts and images I was able to reconstruct, as much as possible, events as they unfolded.

Finally my search led me to a sick old man who decided to break his lifetime of silence on the subject. He promised to reveal the killer's identity and gave me permission to write this book, on one condition – that all names be changed. He told me that the murderer's family still live up the road from my family and that to this day they do not know that their grandfather was a killer.

1

17 January 1907
La Casa sul Poggio
Casentino, Tuscany

The night sky was oppressive with cloud above the uneven mounds of snow around the house. Great thick snowflakes, some as big as a baby's fist, had fallen in flurries all day, lightly at first, then heavily. On either side of the Bruni house the cherry and walnut trees sagged under the snow's weight. By early evening the house, its barn and chestnut drying house, all clustered together on a knoll of flat land midway down the mountainside, looked like three dark smudges on white carpet. Later that evening, the snow stopped falling but the leaden clouds remained and the land was muffled by an intense silence.

During the daylight hours, Artemio Bruni had given the job of checking the rapidly banking snow to his eleven-year-old daughter, Fiamma. She had to make sure that the wall of rising snow didn't completely block the entrance to the house. She kept her shovel and her thick stick propped up close to the front door and every hour or so she would scrape and scoop the snow away. Her mother had told her to do the job in her old wooden clogs then dry them by the fire each time. She did as she was told, even though her feet hung uncomfortably over the back of them, which made her socks sodden and her heels ache. Fiamma's mother said that she looked like a deer gingerly dipping its hooves into snow because of the way she moved: high-stepping delicately, putting her toes down first as she shovelled.

Once darkness closed in, Artemio Bruni kept an eye on the weather himself. Shortly before dinner he opened his front door and stood on the threshold. He looked straight ahead, over his large wheatfield, towards the road that lay five hundred metres from his house. He looked out of habit, knowing he would see nothing and no one. Several kilometres further up, the road disappeared under an umbrella of oak and chestnut branches. Beyond the trees, the road bent to hug the mountainside for about fifteen kilometres until it joined up with the main road that ran along the highest ridges of Casentino's mountains. At this junction, Florence was to the right, after a forty-five-kilometre descent. To the left was the Casentino plateau, arrived at after a thirty-kilometre descent. There the road split again. To the left, Stia and Pratovecchio; to the right, Poppi, Bibbiena and Arezzo.

Still gazing towards the road, Artemio took a deep breath and sighed slowly, his breath a thick cloud of vapour. He shivered and took a step further away from his door, to look at the dark sky. Instinctively he knew that tomorrow would bring more snow. He hitched his pants up a little higher, leaving his fingers in the sash around his waistband to keep them warm. He kept his arms tight against his torso and turned to look left towards the orchard at the side of his house, where the land fell away onto a few hectares of flat, arable land.

Artemio Bruni's house was called Poggio, which means 'hillock' because the knoll it was built upon was too big to be called a mound and too small to be called a plateau. It was known originally as Casa sul Poggio (House on the Knoll) but over the years the name had been shortened to Poggio, and on a clear day or moonlit evening Artemio could see all of his land from his front door. It wasn't a big plot of land – about twenty hectares in all – but it was chestnut-rich. And in food-poor Casentino that meant he'd been blessed while living here. Before turning around to go back inside, he glanced towards the five heavily wooded hectares of chestnut trees beyond the road in front of his house. He felt a fleeting moment of anxiety at the thought of leaving them. Poggio had been his first farm and he'd done exceedingly well with it. But he knew that it was time to let the chestnuts go and try his hand at a bigger farm with more sheep. His family needed cash from the sale of pecorino cheese now, not chestnuts, just to survive.

The distant sound of a strange dog barking made Artemio's eyes shift instantly back to the road. He didn't recognise the bark. Odd – he knew all his neighbours' dogs. He stood for a few seconds, his ear cocked to the black night. His wife, Bruna, called impatiently to him to shut the door or go outside but to get his jacket before he did. He ignored her, scanning the field and the woods but seeing nothing. The bark came again, from further up the road, where it curved and ran under the trees. Echoing clearly against the silent blanket of snow, a second bark joined the first, its pitch high with excitement. He recognised the second dog's bark. It belonged to a family at Il Villaggio, a few kilometres up the road. Il Villaggio was a cluster of seven homes and the Brunis' closest village. Artemio assumed someone new had joined one of the families for an evening around the fire, gatherings the country people called *veglia*.

He turned and walked back inside. His own two dogs, locked inside the barn with the oxen and sheep, were responding now to the echoing howls. As he shut the door and resumed his seat in front of the fire, he decided he would take another look around outside later. There were wolves running in packs in the mountains and they were vicious. His last duty before bed every night was to check his tethered animals; tonight he would be extra vigilant.

Even though the Bruni family had a guest, Artemio picked up his tools and continued to work. A man of quiet determination, Artemio wasn't one to change his habits for others. He kept to his own rhythms, which were in time only with the changing colours of the seasons. These were the white, black and grey months, when the land stood still. And like the trees around him, with their dormant roots deep in the frozen ground, Artemio rested. The bitter cold, generous at least in this, let him do the sedentary, indoor jobs that had been put off during the summer months. Artemio passed a large part of his winter afternoons and evenings in the kitchen mending the tools that had split or worn during the harvest. He soaked his shovels and hoes in pails of water so that their wooden poles would swell and tighten within the metal joints. He fixed the wooden spokes that had jumped their holes on his waxed canvas umbrella. He sharpened his scythe, hatchet and knives. Mostly, though, he made the children's shoes.

On this night Artemio had measured four-year-old Ottavia's feet. Ottavia – called Eighth even though she had been born seventh – had since autumn been wearing her big sister's old clogs. But the brass nails securing the top of the used leather shoe over the wooden sole had come loose. The wood underneath the sole was also splintered and chipped so that Ottavia could no longer walk evenly. He had held her foot up against a length of alder wood and nicked a hole where her toes began and her heels ended. Then he'd hacked the wood down to size. He'd carved the sole into a gentle oblong shape, about one and a half inches thick, and taken the measurements a second time to see where the top of her foot rose to meet her ankle. With a small hammer and many new brass nails, he was now hammering the old soleless shoe over the top of the new clog base. It was a long process that took many hours by the fire, but Artemio enjoyed the retreat the work provided.

Felice, a travelling haberdashery salesman, sat near him. For safety's sake, Casentino's itinerant peddlers had their accommodation settled by the time darkness engulfed the mountains. They either paid an inn for their dinner and bed or they stayed at the last home they sold goods to. Felice, who travelled on foot with his mule loaded with fabric, sheets, thread and buttons, always made la Casa sul Poggio his last call. Every three to four months he stopped by to show his wares to the Brunis and every time he said it was too dark or too cold or too late to make the extra distance (about one kilometre) down the road to the Mazzetti inn. Felice was unfailingly invited to stay.

'Must like my cooking,' Bruna muttered under her breath as she moved towards the kitchen.

Short, fat, with ruddy cheeks and a bulbous nose, Felice was something of an identity among the dozen regular peddlers. This was in part because he had a jocular, self-effacing sense of humour, but also because he was so blatantly unsuited to the physical demands of his job. With huge round sweat stains at his armpits, Felice puffed and wheezed his way around the mountainous roads, selling his wares for less than he should have to make a decent profit. But it was not for his jokes or well-priced sheets that he was most appreciated, it was for the way he had with terracotta. For this, Felice was an invaluable guest.

Bruna owned two copper pots; the rest of her kitchen equipment – plates, pots, jugs, washbasins and roasting dishes – was all terracotta. Often the dishes cracked against each other or the stone sink, and Felice chiselled holes through either side of the damaged pottery so that he could insert a wire to twist and gently pressure it back together again. The wire was never removed.

On his visits, Felice would also bring a flask of red wine from somewhere in the warm valley of Florence. 'For the Brunis,' he would say with a flourish and bang it down heavily on the table. When the flask was out, the younger Bruni children would bring their hands up to their mouths to hide their giggles as they knew that by bedtime Felice would have his 'funny smile on'. They were never sure whether he did it on purpose or if he really did drink that way, but Felice took very deep sips of his wine. So deep that the liquid reached halfway up to his nose. After a while, the wine would stain and he would look as if he had a permanent red smile on his face. 'Felice by name, Felice by nature,' they said. Felice means 'happy'.

By early evening both men leant forward on wooden chairs towards the light of the fire with their work on their laps. They talked with their heads down, sporadically, in low, murmuring voices.

'What was the final count in December?' asked Felice as he reached to pick up some wire.

'Fifty *quintali*,' responded Artemio.

'Hmm, very good. Sell them all?'

'Mostly. Kept some to see us through till April.'

The men were quiet.

'I hear Campo Alto doesn't have any chestnuts.' Felice looked over at Artemio pointedly.

'Doesn't matter,' Artemio said with a small, dismissive shrug. 'There's more land for grain. More pasture for more sheep.'

'A lot of people have asked me if it's true that your brother was told to leave Campo Alto to make way for you,' said Felice, looking back down at his work.

'They should ask me or Sauro, not you.'

'Well? I'm asking you.'

Artemio looked up. 'Sauro was asked to leave because his owners weren't getting their dues. If it wasn't me coming in, it would've been someone else.'

'When do you move?'

'Two weeks, 1 February.' Artemio looked back down to his work.

'Would've been better to leave earlier, no?'

'Humph.' Another small shrug. 'Sauro owes me no favours. He'll leave when his contract tells him to. Earlier or later, it's the same.'

Felice didn't think so, but didn't disagree out loud. He thought about the road that wound up to the junction along the ridge. He knew the new farm, Campo Alto, was on one of the ridge's highest stretches. It would be almost impassable with snow and ice in a couple of weeks. He couldn't imagine herding his family and livestock through the drifts. But then again, maybe there would not be too much to move after all. Most of the goods, grain, seeds, tools and animals belonged to Poggio's owner, not to Artemio. In the end a *mezzadro* farmer possessed nothing but his brute strength. Still, Felice knew the roads better than most and he would never attempt to move a young family in February. He stayed quiet and set a mended plate and washbasin along the fire's hearth.

Around six-thirty, Bruna took the bean *minestrina* off the fire. Her big copper pot, black with soot on the outside and gleaming orange gold on the inside, had been boiling over a soft flame for most of the afternoon. Inside it was a kilo of cannellini beans well covered with water, a handful of dried sage leaves, eight cloves of garlic and a generous sprinkle of salt. By dinnertime, the soup was thick and aromatic.

Bruna Bruni was a small, formidable woman with large breasts that were held in place by her apron. Every day she bound her apron strings above the soft rise of her stomach and half closed her eyes at the relief of having the cumbersome weight of her breasts lifted from her shoulders. It seemed to her that there had not been a day in her adult life that she had not been giving milk. She was forty years old and had given birth to eight children. People often thought she was plumper than she really was, as her shoulders and arms were thick. But she was not a fat woman, she was sturdy. Bruna had a delicate jawline that belied her strength of character.

After a while she called thirteen-year-old Anna away from her game and told her to set the table. She'd been rolling chestnuts with Fiamma, Silvio, Ottavia and baby Pasquale in a game called *birilli*. It was a mix between *bocce* and marbles and at each toss the chestnut made a hollow thunking sound on the wooden floor. The aim was to knock the other players' chestnuts out of the way in order to get as close to the walnut as possible.

Anna folded her long skirt up and away from her feet as she rose to leave the game to help her mother. Of Bruna's eight children, only Anna had inherited her mother's brown eyes. The others, three boys and four girls, all had their father's blue eyes, an uncommon family trait that was often noted and commented upon by neighbours and friends. Anna's face was long and thin like her mother's. She was not beautiful, as Bruna was not beautiful, but she shared her mother's quiet strength. Without ever letting her other children notice, Bruna favoured Anna.

With the same economical movements, Bruna and Anna moved about the kitchen. Anna bundled the brass spoons and glass tumblers up into her arms and placed them neatly by the terracotta bowls. She placed Artemio at the head of the table and Felice at the other end. Bruna put the blackened pot in the table's centre and a coal lamp next to it. Beside Artemio's place she put a pillow-shaped loaf of crusty bread and what was left of their last round of pecorino cheese. There was no need to provide the table with knives as the men had their own and would pull them from their pockets at mealtimes. Artemio's knife was the only object that he would never be without. It was a flick-knife with a five-inch blade. The handle was made from white-grey oxen horn, which gave the grip a textured roughness that Artemio, when he was cold and wet and his hands were slipping, had thanked God for many times.

Bruna called everyone to the table. When Artemio stood, it was Bruna who took his chair from in front of the fire and put it under the table. It was her job to anticipate her husband's every need in the home. Once Artemio had sat down he immediately retrieved his knife. He tucked the loaf of bread under his arm and, with clean upward movements, sliced off thick chunks of it for each of his children and his wife. Felice cut his own bread, once Artemio had passed the loaf down to him. Artemio crouched over his plate, his head bent and his shoulders hunched, with both elbows on the table. He held his bread in his left hand and his spoon in his right, putting food into his mouth quickly, with no heed to the noise he made. The children ate in a similar way, gathering speed as they went, as though surprised by how hungry they were.

The table ran almost the length of the room. It was made to seat six, but when the whole Bruni family was present, it seated ten. Bruna and six of her children sat on two long planks of chestnut wood that Artemio had fashioned into benches by placing them on upturned barrels. The kitchen was neither large nor small – about seven steps wide and eight steps long. However, with nine people in it, the air was hot, humid and stuffy. The room smelt musty with the odour of unwashed bodies in stale clothes. A dank smell of wet wool also hung in the air, along with the aroma of beans and a toasty smell of roasted chestnuts.

There was one window above the sink and it was about the size of four men's hands placed together to form a square. It was rarely opened. Consequently, as the temperature dropped outside and rose inside, thick condensation formed on the glass and ran in rivulets down the panes. By morning, once the warm bodies had gone to bed and the fire had died down, the condensation frosted into a sheet of ice so thick that the window was frozen shut for most of the day.

Once the bean soup was finished, Bruna rose to get a basket full of yellow apples, picked that summer. They smelt syrupy-sweet after their time inside the larder, which had served to mature their flavour inside their skins. They were slightly soft with age, with black spots like moles on their skins. The Brunis ate them with walnuts, pecorino cheese and bread. They finished their meal with roasted chestnuts. They would eat the apples and walnuts till they ran out. From then on, usually around early March, there would be only chestnuts on the table after dinner.

Little Ottavia rose first from the table. She walked around to Felice and pointed to his mouth. 'You have your funny smile on now!' she said shyly.

'Ragghhh!' roared Felice, making his face fearsome as he grabbed her around the waist and hoisted her onto his lap. She squealed but made no move to escape.

'Where did Mario get to tonight?' asked Felice, referring to the Brunis' eldest son. 'Seems to me that young Mario might have found a signorina?'

Bruna glanced at Artemio, who kept his eyes on his hands. He was cleaning his nails with his knife. As a rule Artemio and Bruna didn't speak much. They looked at each other and the words seemed to pass silently between them.

You answer, Bruna was thinking.

'Don't know. Gone to *veglia*,' Artemio said.

'So I'm right then: Mario has found a signorina?' Felice shifted Ottavia slightly to one side so that he could lean forward for his cup and take another deep sip of wine.

'Maybe,' Artemio said. He wanted Bruna to answer now.

'I have it in my mind that he's been passing a lot of time with the boys from Podervecchio,' offered Bruna.

'Probably acquiring a taste for cards.' Felice intuited that he should leave the matter. He leant forward slightly so that he could breathe in the smell of the little girl's hair. She smelt of burnt firewood and apples.

Bruna sighed and pushed herself off the bench to start gathering the plates. It was the sign for each child to begin their before-bed chores. Anna helped her mother clear the table while sixteen-year-old Maria led Fiamma, Silvio and baby Pasquale over to the front door. She plucked their coats from their hooks on the wall and helped the children into them while they pulled on their woolly bonnets and hats. She took Artemio's outdoor glass lamp, lit it and led the children outside. At the back of the house, where the land plunged away down the mountainside, was the manure square. It looked like a big Roman bath, except that inside there was animal manure mixed with hay. The children hung their bottoms over the edge and relieved themselves.

Artemio moved his chair back to the fire while the others took turns outside. Felice went out last and then he too retired upstairs. He shared a double bed in the boys' room with nine-year-old Silvio and nineteen-year-old Mario. The four girls slept together in the room at the end of the corridor upstairs. No one undressed – it was too cold. Everyone slipped off their shoes and climbed into bed fully clothed.

Artemio gazed at the flames and absently listened to the house gradually grow quiet. He could hear the girls' muffled chatter from their bed while Bruna wrapped little Pasquale's bottom up in rags in front of the fire. Baby Pasquale went to the manure pit only for potty practice, as he was not yet free of the cotton strips that kept the bed he shared with Artemio and Bruna dry. Once Pasquale was wrapped and dressed again, Bruna carried him upstairs to breastfeed. She did not pause by her husband with Pasquale in her arms as Artemio did not kiss, hold or show any other physical affection to his children.

Artemio linked his fingers above his head and stretched his arms high. His thoughts drifted to Mario. He did not like his son going out and he especially did not like not knowing where his son was. But he was a young adult now and Artemio could not hold him back. The trouble with Mario was his temper. He held within him a fury that was blind to circumstance and reason. Just as a man can sense when a dog is about to attack, a man could sense a threat in Mario. Mostly people were stiff and awkward around him. But the boy was a worker. And in a society where men were judged by their physical strength and their ability to work hard, Mario had the district's respect. Artemio was at once proud of his son and concerned about him.

At the sound of Bruna's footsteps coming back down the wooden stairs, Artemio grunted and rose from his chair. He unwound the sash at his waist and rewound it again, three times, and tighter. Bruna moved silently past him into the kitchen, where she bent to pull some pails out from under the sink. She threw Pasquale's dirty rags into them while Artemio walked to the door for his jacket and hat. He picked up the lantern and went outside.

The cold air hit his cheeks like a slap on the face. Two steps away from the house and the snow was deeper, so that he had to wade. Most Casentino houses had stone stairs outside the kitchen that led down to the stable; that way the farmers could keep their animals under the house. With the animals so close, they could hear from their beds the scraping hooves or bellows of discomfort if one of the oxen came loose. The oxen had long horns with sharp points and were tied to the troughs with loose chains around their necks. If they came free they wandered about in the open stalls and stabbed one another. Unfortunately Artemio did not have the luxury of a downstairs stable, though he looked forward to it at the new farm. To reach his barn and stable he had to walk thirty metres down the side of the house, past the chestnut drying house along an undulating track, to where the barn sat opposite the orchard. His movements disturbed the big brown owl that lived under Poggio's rafters. It flew off towards the woods, pushing its huge wings through the air, sounding like someone vigorously shaking out a sheet.

As Artemio rounded the house, a pile of snow fell from a walnut branch and ploffed softly on the ground beside him. He could hear the stream running stealthily down the hill towards Stia, and from the barn came the loud braying of Felice's mule.

Artemio stopped short at the barn's entrance. Around the door and up the side of it were several sets of footprints. Either one person had walked around the barn many times, or several people had recently been inside. Artemio thought of his dogs and wondered why they had not barked and, indeed, were not barking still. He raised his lantern to shoulder height and peered down, puzzled.

He reached out to the latch and found that it was raised. With his fingertips he pushed open the door, then he stepped inside the barn's darkness.

※

Bruna was collecting ash from the fire and settling the flames for the night when she heard a scratching sound at the front door. Her back bent over the hearth, she turned her head to listen. It came again, as though an animal were trying to find its way into the warmth of the house. She thought that one of Artemio's dogs had been let out of the barn and had reached the house before him. She finished her work and straightened her back. The scratching changed to a pound – once, like something dense falling against the door.

She stepped quickly yet warily towards the door and opened it a crack, looking out into the night, then down. She let out a small, soundless gasp and pulled the door wide. Artemio slumped inside and rolled onto his back.

'Oh, Signore! Oh, Signore! Oh, Lord! Oh, Lord!' Bruna said softly as she fell to her knees. Quickly, fervently, she made the sign of the cross on her chest before she touched her husband.

'Holy Mary, Mother of God, what happened?' she said as she placed her hand gently across his forehead as though feeling for a fever. His eyes were open and fixed on her with an intensity she found more frightening than the blood coming from the back of his head. She ran her hand up over the top of his head, gingerly making her way down to the back of his neck. There was a gash – neat, long and warm in her palm.

'Felice! Felice!' she screamed.

Bruna could feel her blood-soaked hands begin to tremble as she pushed herself off the floor to find a towel for Artemio's head. She knew she had to stop the bleeding and make Artemio warm and dry. The blood at the top of his collar had begun to freeze. The sleeves of his padded jacket were soaked, his pants too. His hands were purple and stiff from the cold. Bruna realised then that Artemio had crawled along the path to reach her.

By the time Felice was down the stairs Artemio's eyes had begun to roll back into his skull and still he lay in the open doorway.

'Oh my God. Oh my God ... Artemio. Artemio. What have you done?' Felice cried. He ran his hands almost roughly over Artemio's shoulders and chest, as if he could revive him with a strong touch.

'Grab his ankles and help me pull him in,' Felice said to Bruna in a fierce whisper. He squatted by Artemio's head and slipped his hands under the injured man's armpits. Together they dragged him into the house. Bruna closed the door and slid shut the latch.

With Felice's help, she was able to remove Artemio's jacket, sweater, shoes, socks, sash, pants and long johns. They put him into a dry, worn jacket. While Felice carried him up the stairs, Bruna turned back the bed and laid an extra blanket inside it. Once Artemio was on the bed, Bruna placed his hands across his chest. She folded and tucked the blanket around him, cocooning him inside the covers beside baby Pasquale. Then she folded another towel behind his neck and tied yet another one behind that, around his head.

Once they had done all they could, Felice left her to go back to bed. The children had slept through the whole ordeal and Bruna knew that she would have to endure this night alone. Felice had not even suggested going to fetch a doctor – they both knew that he would die of exposure before he reached the nearest one at Stia. Nor had he proposed going out to the barn to investigate the source of Artemio's injury. They understood the danger and in unspoken agreement remained locked indoors.

Bruna sat by her husband's bedside all night. She prayed that he would open his eyes and call for something. But he lay still, the colour slowly draining from his face, and she knew that he was dying.

After a while she went downstairs and placed his clothes on the back of a chair in front of the fire. She took several of the jackets that hung on the hooks by the front door and went back upstairs again. Bruna wrapped herself in the jackets and laid another one across her knees.

She looked up at the ceiling and realised that the wind had picked up because the snow was coming through from outside. The gusts blew it through the slates of the roof onto the wooden planks beneath them. Every now and then a powdery cloud of snow would fall on Artemio's face and she would rise to brush it away.

Throughout that long night Bruna's thoughts kept returning to the words *la nuca, la nuca* – the nape, the nape – where the hardness of her husband's skull gave way to the softness of his neck. He had been hit just once, but with such force it had split open the back of his head. She had always loved that part of him. He had a swirl, like a cowlick, at the nape of his neck and she'd teased him about it, saying that when God made him it was as if He had dipped His finger into Artemio's hair and twirled out a snail. It was where she let her fingers rest and roam when he lay on top of her. It was the first place she looked when her babies were born, to see if they had inherited their father's swirl. It was where the killer had struck her lover.

By morning Artemio was dead.

2

July 1906

Bruna woke to a blue dawn light that had begun to lift the darkness from her bedroom. For a few minutes she stared into it blankly, while her senses tuned into the morning. Her limbs felt heavy and her eyes gritty; it had been a long night. When Artemio stirred beside her, she remembered that tomorrow the harvest would begin and that today would be one of the busiest days of her year.

Raising herself onto her elbow, she looked down for baby Pasquale, asleep somewhere in the bed. During the night his little body slipped between the mounds and furrows that were formed by his parents' heavier bodies in the cornhusks that stuffed the mattress. She saw that he had ended up lying diagonally across the bed with his feet on Artemio's chest. Both father and son snored, Pasquale with little airy breaths that were miniatures of his father's big snorts.

Bruna pushed the sheet gently off her body and swung her bare legs up and over the edge of the mattress so that she could push herself out of bed. Although she did her best to move quietly, the cornhusks crackled anyway. She slipped her cotton dress over her shift and buttoned it up while sliding her feet into her boots. Her waist-length hair, formerly a solid inky black but now flecked with iron strands, was braided down both sides of her face. She looped the plaits back into a bun and secured them with a headscarf. Then she pulled her apron over her head and deftly tied its strings.

Carefully tiptoeing out of the bedroom, she glanced over her shoulder at her husband and son. She did not want to disturb them as she could achieve so much more at this time of day if they slept a while longer. Once downstairs she picked up her shawl, the copper water jug and copper pot, and went out to the stream at the back of the house. There the light was soft on the orchard, the sheep in their summer pen still more asleep than awake. The only sounds were the cascading stream and the twitter and buzz from some of the more industrious birds and insects.

Along the side of the house the dirt path was hard and dry under Bruna's feet. So far it had been a hot summer with only a few splashes of rain in early July. Not enough to affect the grain, just enough to fatten the zucchini and tomatoes. They'd need much more for the chestnuts.

The stream was three hundred metres from the house, at the bottom of a ravine with a treacherous track that ran like a diagonal sword slash down the side of the mountain. Bruna paused at the top of it and passed the pot over to the hand that held the jug so that she had one hand free to grab onto the tree trunks as she skidded down.

At the water's edge she crouched to put the water containers into the current. She bunched her skirts in between her knees and rolled up her sleeves so that she could splash her face without wetting her dress. Even though it was midsummer the stream was ice cold, having bubbled up from an underground spring further up the mountain. She bent forward on her haunches to let the water run through her fingers, enjoying the sensation of the liquid coursing through her hands. She often did that – enjoyed the feel of things. She would fluff freshly shorn lambs' wool, ball it tightly and marvel at its springy lightness. Or stir through baskets of chestnuts to feel their smooth, dense skins clacking against each other. She crushed spindly broom brush and palmed its dryness. When she felt these objects she looked distant, as if she were not thinking of what she touched. But Bruna was not being vague, she was inside her senses. Everything that she handled gave her deep pleasure because it all had a purpose in her life. All that she owned and ate, nature provided. She was in awe of it and often let it absorb her.

Eventually she sat back on a flat rock and let her mind wander to Primo. She did this every morning when her mind was clear. He was her first baby and had he not been taken by tuberculosis two years ago, he would have been twenty-one this year. Bruna had been nineteen years old when he was born and he had been nineteen years old when he died. Babies were always dying in the farming community, she knew that. They were buried without funerals because there was no time to baptise them. But she'd never lost a baby. Her Primo had been a fully grown man when he died and she felt the grief from losing him like a fist around her heart. Sometimes, such as when she looked down the table at all her children's faces as they ate their dinner and his was missing, the fist squeezed her heart. At other times, mostly during the day when she was busy, the pressure eased a little.

After picturing Primo for a while, her thoughts wandered to the day ahead. Last night she had kneaded five kilos of flour and she would add a further five kilos to that dough this morning. It would swell until midday, ready then to divide up into fourteen loaves of bread. Together with a goose, the bread would feed the dozen or so neighbours who were coming to help with the threshing of the wheat this week.

The sheaves would be brought up to the *aia* (farmyard) in front of the house and put onto the ground in a big oval. When she climbed inside it, the walls of grain made her feel as though she were inside a giant trough. *Tung, tung, tung* went the sheaves as they hit the planks of wood placed on the ground inside the oval, so that the wheat separated from the chaff. The husks flew into everyone's hair, mouth, eyes and stuck like mosquitoes to their sweat. But nobody minded because they were all working in the trough together. Bruna's favourite part was when someone started singing and all the voices would 'tru la la a li la la' across the fields.

Then her sons would carry the kitchen table and benches out to the orchard and put them under the shadiest pear trees. Bruna would set it with a sheet, the platter of boiled goose meat and a huge pot of broth full of little pasta squares. She'd stuff the goose's neck with breadcrumbs, parsley and salt, and its meat would be moist and fatty. The goose itself, plump and angry, was in the yard right now, ready to be killed later today.

After her neighbours had devoured the goose and its broth, they would help themselves to potatoes. Bruna planned to boil them in their jackets so that they kept their flavour; she would peel them just before serving with a sprinkle of salt and a splash of olive oil. Some of the bread she was making today would be soaked in water for the *panzanella* salad. She'd squeeze the water out so that the bread looked like a big squashed sponge, then crumble it into diced tomatoes, cucumber, sliced basil, lettuce, onions, salt and olive oil. To finish, the threshers would eat cheese and plums together with slices of her bread. Then they'd rest a little, till the sun was not so high, while the boys from Podervecchio sneaked glances at Maria, and Bruna prayed that Artemio would not notice.

Once the Brunis' grain was threshed and ready for the mill, the family would move along to the next farm to thresh their grain in return. There would be a goose feast there too, though perhaps it would be cooked in a different way, maybe according to some time-honoured family tradition that improved on the *pastina* or the broth. Sometimes the goose was cut into pieces and cooked for hours with chopped onions, celery and carrots, then the sauce – rich and fatty – was served over thick strips of pasta. Bruna looked forward to the season. It was the summer of every Tuscan farmer – moving from one farm to the next to help with the grain, threshing and feasting.

As if to remind her of her chores, the church bell up the hill chimed slowly six times. Her containers full and Primo remembered, Bruna walked slowly back up the ravine, the weight of the water at her sides helping to anchor her feet to the steep path. The sun was slightly higher now and the air held the promise of a hot day.

When Bruna opened the kitchen door, Artemio was already at the sink, ready for the water with his razor in hand. He grew his whiskers into a black handlebar moustache, as thick as three fingers in the middle and upturned and wiry towards the end. It was the fashion of the day and Artemio liked to trim and turn it every morning before breakfast. He'd already lit the fire, so Bruna hung the copper pot onto its hook over the flames while Artemio poured some water from the jug into a terracotta bowl in the sink. He propped his small mirror on the windowsill, pushed back his sleeves, humped his back and started his shave.

In summer Artemio had a dark tan that stopped starkly at the bottom of his throat and midway up his sinewy forearms. He was short enough not to have to bend his head when he passed under the doorway's low lintels, and he had a wiry rather than muscly body. He also possessed an unusually long neck and bandy legs with a barrel-shaped chest in between. All in all, Artemio Bruni did not look like a strong man and that had earnt him the nickname 'Gambine', or 'Littlelegs'. This was not a nickname his wife or children used, but a name that his friends called him when they talked about him or beckoned to him at the marketplace.

'*E come va il nostro Gambine oggi?* And how is our Littlelegs today?' they would say as they stopped Artemio with a clap on his back. Or 'Whatever you do, don't ask Littlelegs to carry that or his legs will snap like toothpicks.' Artemio's nickname did not bother him because everyone in Casentino had one. He even considered himself quite lucky because, as far as nicknames went, Gambine wasn't that bad. His friends Bugiardino (Littleliar) and Furbo (Sly) hated their names and could not even remember where they had got them, though they suspected that their big brothers were in some way responsible. Bizzine (Tantrums) and Veleno (Poison) had earnt their names because of their reactions to a perceived injustice while working in the fields. Mostly, the names stuck because of a well-known incident, as when Botte (Punches) started swinging at a man after too much wine, and

Mestolino (Woodenspoon) was seen running after his son waving a wooden spoon. Physical defects (the men were most sensitive about these) had labelled Testasecca (Dryhead), Boccaccia (Uglymouth) and Culino (Littlebum) for life.

When Bruna first met Artemio he'd been dubbed Littlelegs for some time, but she didn't know about it until they were almost married. The name didn't offend her, she knew it could have been far worse; and besides, when they had first met it was not his legs she noticed but his light blue eyes. They had a band of yellow around the iris, as though God couldn't decide what colour to make them, blue or yellow. It was an odd colour for a Casentino man and one that demanded closer inspection. Whenever she did come within close range of his eyes, she found they were staring into her own in an intense, serious way that she liked.

She had been sent to the tiny village of Omomorto (five houses and three barns) to help the Bruni family collect their chestnuts off the forest floor. She was seventeen years old and had gone with her fifteen-year-old sister in return for two meals a day. Her own family had no chestnut trees, only a small farm on the damp side of the mountain that produced barely enough food for her brothers and sisters. Artemio's family had no farm but a rented house that came with several hundred chestnut trees. At that time Artemio was twenty and looking to leave home to take on his own farm, and Bruna did not doubt that he was looking for a young wife to go with it.

Their courting officially started one month later when all the chestnuts were on their trays over fires in their drying house, and by then Bruna's curiosity about Artemio was overwhelming. She thought about the way he set his jaw and tightened his mouth when she looked him in the eye. She wondered what he was thinking when he did that. What she saw on the outside was a sinewy man with a reliable gaze. What she saw on the inside was a solidity that would never mellow into laziness.

When another month had passed and the chestnuts were dry, they found that their affection for each other was sound. Before he asked her to marry him, he told her that he liked that she was quiet, a little reserved and not too gay. He said he liked the way she ran her fingers along the pleat of her skirt and examined the straw of the basket with her hands. He did not tell her that he loved her; she thought that he would later.

By Christmas that year, Artemio had asked her father for her hand and, when given it, he brought her family a compressed fruit and nut cake from Siena – a *panforte* – as was the custom for the family of one's fiancée.

'Tell Fiamma to take the sheep into the woods today. She must take the hatchet and chop as many branches as she can. She can leave them there to dry, we'll get them later. Maria must retie some of those tomatoes onto their poles. I'll take Silvio and Mario with me.' Artemio had thrust his jaw forward to accommodate his sweeping blade and his instructions sounded contorted. 'You have to collect the oxen's manure for the *aia* and get it ready.'

Bruna went into the cool room, which also doubled as the cheese-making room, to retrieve last night's risen dough. She had already started on the oxen's manure. It had to be prepared well in advance of threshing day. The black dung pats were blended with water to make a paste that dried like waterproof tar. It was spread inside the threshing trough so that not one grain of wheat was lost. Bruna did not respond to Artemio's orders and he didn't expect her to. She would pass them on to the children, along with her own.

Climbing into the oven was not Ottavia's favourite job. But at four years old she was the only one who could fit inside to clean it. The oven was in the side wall of the house, near where the rabbits and chickens were kept in a little fenced-off area, beyond the cheese room. Its entrance was about the size of an open Bible and it was Ottavia's responsibility to sweep it out before baking every week. Once inside the oven, she could move around in a crouch, lie down and almost stand up. One day she would be too big for the job and it would fall to baby Pasquale, but for now any work that required a small body was Ottavia's. She cleaned the oven without complaining, but dragged her heels when it was time to go in.

'Go on now, in you go,' said Bruna, pushing Ottavia towards the oven and passing her a small, tightly bound bunch of twigs to sweep with.

'Yoo-whooo … *Buon giorno*! I have blackberry jam! But it's only for good little girls,' came a voice from behind Bruna and Ottavia. Signora Mazzetti, Bruna's friend, had arrived early to help with the baking.

'Can I have some when I've finished?' asked Ottavia, pausing on top of an upturned wicker basket that was put in front of the oven for her to step on.

'You can, Ottavia, but get *in* now,' Bruna said with a little shove. She then turned to hug and kiss her friend.

'*Buon giorno*, Signora Mazzetti,' she greeted her with a smile. Even though she'd known the elderly woman all her life and loved her like a mother, she used the formal mode of address. It reflected her utmost respect for her. '*Che bella!* How delicious! From the woods behind your house?'

'Yes, and from the bushes down near Podervecchio – found them before anyone else did. Ha!'

'Mamma! Can I have the jam on bread?' The little voice reverberated around the terracotta oven, as though she were in a tomb.

'Ottavia, if you don't start sweeping, there'll be nothing left for you by the time the boys come back!' Bruna took her friend's arm and guided her through the cheese room and into the kitchen.

Signora Fausta Mazzetti and her husband, Marcello, lived one kilometre down the road and were the Brunis' closest neighbours. They were also the Brunis' closest friends, even though both were old enough to be their grandparents. Signora Mazzetti had malt-coloured liver spots on her face, and her spine was so bent that just a glance at her would make the younger girls pull back their shoulders and stand up straight. In the kitchen, Bruna cast about for a place for her guest to sit down, as all the planks of wood that doubled as benches were lined with rising loaves of bread, ready to be balanced on her shoulder and carried to the oven.

'*Si-eh! Lasciami fare.* As if! Leave me alone, I don't like sitting.' She waved Bruna away before spotting baby Pasquale lying on a coat in the corner. He cooed softly when he saw her, recognising her immediately. With a quickness that belied her age, Signora Mazzetti bent down to scoop him up in her arms.

'How's my boy?' She squeezed the baby's cheeks before loudly kissing them. Baby Pasquale giggled. 'Now, what did I want to say?' She had a habit of prefacing her speech like this. It was her way of stopping anyone from moving the conversation along before she had had her say. Bruna was used to it, so she said nothing.

'You look tired, my dear girl.'

'Silvio was up during the night with earache again.'

'Did you warm the olive oil inside the walnut shell before pouring it in?'

'Yes, and it did seem to calm the pain.'

'Well, I'll have a look at him this afternoon. And how's that goose? Fat? I hate plucking them. Horrible feathers, so much worse than chickens, stick like mortar and cement. When are you making the *pastina*?'

'After lunch, when all the bread is done.' Bruna's body sagged a little. She was stirring a pot of onion soup over the fire – six onions, five carrots, spinach, beans and five sticks of celery in water with salt and wild herbs. She would serve it on top of the last of the old bread for lunch. On weekdays lunch and dinner were always soup and always seasonal. Whatever was ready to be pulled out of the vegetable garden went into the minestrone. Ricotta cheese and blackberry jam, thanks to Signora Mazzetti, spread on top of the fresh bread would follow.

'Good, I'll come back to help.'

'Maria will be here. But, yes, thank you.'

'Hmm, what else was there?' Signora Mazzetti said, putting Pasquale down. 'Oh, yes. I heard Artemio's brother will be served his contract cancellation on the Campo Alto farm by July's end,' Signora Mazzetti went on, smoothing Pasquale's sweater. She did not look at Bruna. She did not need to. She'd always been able to anticipate Bruna's reactions. From the moment she'd held her pink newborn body in her hands she'd felt as if she could almost read her mind. About forty years ago, when she'd lost all hope that her own children would be conceived, she'd cut the cord between Bruna and her mother and it was as though she'd connected it to herself. She'd delivered other babies before but had never experienced the inexplicable rush of love that she'd felt for this one. Examining her body for imperfections, she'd found a large black mole on Bruna's shoulderblade. Turning to Bruna's mother, who was at the time her neighbour and dear friend, she'd shown her the black mark. *'Chi ha il neo e non lo vede ha fortuna e non lo crede.* Who has the mole where you cannot see it will have luck but won't believe it,' she'd said. It was an ancient saying and one that she'd always believed.

'Let's call her Bruna,' Grazia had said. Bruna means dark and Signora Mazzetti had thought the name perfect.

When Bruna was little, Signora Mazzetti had kept a sharp eye on her, till she inherited a house from a barren aunt and had to move away. When she'd heard that young Bruna was ready to wed a man looking for a farm to rent, she'd used her influence and found them Poggio, bringing Bruna right back to where Signora Mazzetti felt she belonged. Close to her.

Bruna had thought the idea was perfect and she was grateful to Signora Mazzetti. Her own mother would be too far away for regular visits, but now she would have her honorary mamma just next door. It made her feel as though her mole really had brought her good fortune, as Signora Mazzetti was no ordinary woman. Not only did she possess influence, she was blessed with considerable spiritual powers, the evidence of which Bruna had lived with for most of her life.

Born the seventh daughter of seven girls, Signora Fausta Mazzetti held a rare and revered position of birth, a place that assured her special powers of healing. Called a *settimina* – little seventh – Signora Mazzetti could claim as her birthright the battle against the devil and the ills that he brought with him. Witches, warlocks, wizards and ghosts were a part of everyday Tuscan life and few knew how to recognise and deal with them. Authentic *settiminas* were sought after for this practice and were most uncommon, so much so that certain other less gifted women in Casentino claimed the birthright for themselves. These counterfeits insisted that being born on the seventh day of the seventh month sufficed. But they were false claims: a woman had to be born seventh of seven girls to be blessed with the canny vision needed to thwart sorcerers. Not exactly a crone, fortune teller, exorcist or midwife, Signora Mazzetti was a woman with a natural gift for making people feel better.

Some called her a magician because of her incantations and chants, but she felt nervous with this explanation and was more comfortable with the understanding that she used God's authority to cure and His guidance to procure her medicines. Without a doubt the parish priest was an effective weapon against *il malocchio* – the evil eye – the most frequent of curses; after all, in his devotional presence one was as close to God as one could get. However, Signora Mazzetti was consulted more frequently than the clergy because a priest's prayers were not accompanied by an elixir, poultice or tonic. Nor would he stay up late to pour olive oil into a bowl of water held by a woman hexed by a jealous neighbour. If the oil separated she was cursed, and a priest could not murmur commands in a tongue no one understood till the oil's slick green surface coalesced again and the woman was free of possession.

All of Casentino agreed that the monks, of course, were excellent medicinal gardeners. But here, too, Signora Mazzetti was more readily consulted as no one could afford their prices. Nor could anyone take the time away from their land to travel up to the furthest reaches of the Alps to their monastery, La Verna. The *settimina* above Stia did not pass sentence on afflictions that were *perhaps* caused by sin, either. Signora Mazzetti knew of no distinction between spiritual, holistic and homeopathic work. It was all one and the same for her. She believed that sickness was natural and that diseases either developed of their own accord or were symptoms of the devil's presence. The sick could hardly be blamed for that, she said. With her keen gaze she could penetrate the most hidden evil and pronounce a cure.

Furthermore, she was kind of heart and accepted whatever payment her clients could afford. A *grappolo* of tomatoes, a sack of potatoes, a pair of knitted socks: the cost a fair exchange for the disappearance of worms, fevers, fits, boils or styes. A cabbage was nothing compared with the peace of mind the dissolution of a hex or the banishment of an ill omen from your fields brought. Above all, Signora Mazzetti was one of them – she talked and thought like the farmers. Besides, as there were no doctors or hospitals for many miles, she was all they had.

Bruna Bruni did not know how she would have managed without her dear neighbour. Signora Mazzetti had been unable to save Primo's life but she had made certain that Mario's life was spared. She had rescued him from pneumonia when he was fifteen years old, prescribing 'angel's water' – the urine of the smallest child in the family. He had pulled out of his fever within a week of drinking it. Bruna shared everything with Signora Mazzetti because she, too, was a very superstitious woman and fervently believed in the world of evil spirits, as had her mother. Signora Mazzetti had taught Bruna how to take the proper precautions against the witches that waited by her doorway, biding their time until they could sneak into her home. She advised hanging a fir tree branch on the front door. Before entering, a witch is required to count all the branch's needles and, as this takes a long time, she loses her patience and leaves. One day Signora Mazzetti even climbed down to the stream to where Bruna collected her water and secreted into the rocks a pair of scissors to cut away the bad water, so that only the good flowed into Bruna's containers. All the Bruni children, at Signora Mazzetti's behest, chewed raw garlic. It kept illness and Satan away. Bruna felt incredibly fortunate to have such a wise woman as her closest friend and was indebted to her.

Bruna, however, would never be able to repay Signora Mazzetti. For, what the elderly woman wanted, Bruna was not able to give. From the cradle to the altar Signora Mazzetti had watched the child change from a reedy grasshopper of a girl who sang blissfully, into a thick-set matron whose songs reflected melancholy. She had hoped that by being near her she could help Bruna avoid the weariness that jaded a woman's life. Her prayers had been that Bruna would match herself with someone more like her own Marcello, a husband who would feed her needs, intuit her feelings. Artemio was a good man, but he did not treasure Bruna the way he ought to. She'd seen him turn away from Bruna when the load she carried was too heavy. When her eyes called for rest, Artemio was blind. Life was snatching Bruna's joy and replacing it with exhaustion and exasperation as she struggled to feed her family. There was little Bruna could do to stop the changes inside her caused by tiredness and that was what Signora Mazzetti wanted above all other things.

'Losing a contract for one's farm is distressing news,' Signora Mazzetti said slowly, looking up to see that Bruna's hands had stopped moving over the fire. 'Especially when it's a relative.'

'How do you know this?' Even after all these years Bruna was still amazed at the things her friend found out. The farmers and their children were illiterate, so news travelled only by word of mouth.

'I mean no offence to your husband, but his brother has not cared well for Campo Alto. That's common knowledge.'

'But the contract cancellation. How do you know about that?'

'Ah. My Marcello saw Campo Alto's manager at Stia market and he mentioned there would be big changes up at the farm by July's end. You know the law – a farmer must be told to vacate his farm by 31 July. His words could mean only that. They're out.'

Bruna left the fireplace and moved towards the bread. So, Artemio's brother was to be evicted from his farm. With nowhere to go it was likely he would move his wife and children in with his parents. Signore and Signora Bruni still lived in their rented room in the house at Omomorto, on the main road between Stia and Consuma. The hectares of chestnuts that their children had grown up with were no longer theirs to care for. Once Artemio, his brother, Sauro, and his two older sisters had moved out, the owners had taken the trees from the elderly couple and moved a large young family into the room upstairs. A wretched life awaited Sauro if he shifted everyone back in with his parents, as there was nothing to harvest or farm. Sadness swelled in Bruna's heart. As she bent down to pat the loaves, she shook her head and clicked her tongue. Artemio would be furious with his little brother.

3

Artemio Bruni put his sickle into the hook on his sash and looked across his wheatfield to see how much work still needed to be done. From the look of the chunks cut into his two-hectare field they were making good time. The early-morning summer sun had swollen into a fiery ball above Poggio's mountain, lighting up his field but leaving everything underneath its reach in dark green shadow. The ridges to the mountain's side smoothed down to the Casentino valley, then rolled one after the other into a muted lavender horizon. Neat rows of olive trees, ploughed earth and corn stalks cross-hatched the slopes around Stia, visible from where he stood.

Artemio pulled his straw hat down over his eyes and looked towards Mario, Maria and Silvio. The four of them were working in a loose line, each with a sickle in one hand.

In their other hand they held bundles of wheat, the sheaves long and dry. When their arms were full they laid their bundles on the ground and moved on to the next area of wheat to be cut.

Artemio rubbed the palms of his hands together to ease the tension in his fingers and turned to look behind him for his girls. Fiamma and Anna were to follow him at a distance but they often became distracted and dawdled, as they did not want to be scolded for coming within striking range of the deadly little scythes. It was the girls' job to tie the sheaves together as the harvesting quartet moved through the field. In their hands they held plaited lengths of dampened straw. The girls would kneel beside the sheaves, tie them together then leave them in rows along the ground. Tomorrow the sheaves would be gathered and placed together, four at a time, stalks in the middle, to form a cross. Then, from the field's centre, a wide pyramid of wheat would grow to be pitchforked onto a cart and moved closer to the house for threshing.

Artemio guessed that the girls had found a common field spider – the big, black kind, with legs as long and thin as a strand of hair. They had squatted down to look at it, their heads almost touching in concentration. They sang loudly:

Capra santa
capra santa
strappi una gamba
e dammi l'acqua

Holy goat
Holy goat
Rip off a leg
And give me some water

They squealed when the spider, which now had one leg less, squirted a drop of water onto Anna's palm, as they knew it would. Anna made to smear the liquid onto Fiamma's face, but the smaller girl knew it was coming and darted off quickly with another squeal. She ran like a wind-up tin soldier, straightbacked, her legs scuffing out in front of her so as not to kick off her clogs. Anna didn't bother to give chase. She stayed in a crouch and set the crippled spider free, though she was tempted to pull off the rest of its legs too.

Artemio unhooked his sickle and bent back into his work. He felt much lighter than he had last night when Bruna had told him the news of Sauro, the implications of which had become apparent immediately. No mercy was ever shown to an ejected *mezzadro*. From Carrara to Florence to Siena to Pisa, very few owned their own farms. All were *mezzadros*, sharecroppers who paid to their masters half of everything that was grown, bred or sold. Everyone had to kiss another man's dirt, and if you didn't, you were cast aside. There would be no more chances for Sauro; at least, not in Tuscany. He would be forced to live with his mother and father, and he and his children would be scavengers, foragers for grass, mushrooms, walnuts and firewood, plunderers of the woods at night. Sauro and his boys could hire themselves out for manual labour that paid meals only, but they would have no money and no way of making it. A *mezzadro* might always be at the mercy of his landowner, but could always scratch something out of the garden for his dinner table. Not so for *pigionali* (pigeons) the renters, the poorest of the poor Tuscans who managed only to rent a house, rather than a farm. Or *prigionali*, as they were nicknamed – 'prisoners', jailed within their own poverty. The gossipmongers in Casentino would lose no time in gabbling about his brother, as to whether he'd been dismissed because he was useless, disobedient or in debt. Artemio suspected that Sauro was being accused of all three. He was weak and had always been so. Four sons in whom he could see no fault ruled him. A father who could not command was not fit to raise sons, and now their parents would be dragged down into his misery. His mother and father had been doing well enough too, since losing their chestnut trees, surviving on the sale of a chicken, a rabbit or eggs on the steps of Stia's church of a Sunday. They earnt their rent money mainly through washing for Poggio's owners. His mother smashed the ice with a rock and washed the petticoats, crocheted towels, bloomers and sheets till her chilblains erupted in pustules and bled. His father picked up the washing and dropped it off in his wheelbarrow. But with six extra mouths to feed, the washing and church-market money would never be enough.

These thoughts had assailed Artemio throughout the night, churning his guts till Bruna had told him he may as well just get up and make a start on the harvest. He felt better now. Out in the field, his anxiety had fallen away with the wheat stalks. There was nothing he could do to help his parents or his brother, so he let the wheat's gritty smell, the dry rustle of the husks as they willowed together in his arms, fill him with peace. The grain in his hands would help feed his family for another year and bringing it in never failed to cheer him. Half the crop was his, the other half his owner's. As though sensing their father's mood, Maria and Silvio called to each other, laughing at something as they scythed. A feeling of bounty and wellbeing flowed through them all.

It was eight in the morning and they'd already been scything for four hours. Bruna had joined them to reap in the moonlight, but had left at daybreak to tend to Ottavia and the waking baby, the animal feed and breakfast. At the sound of her call, '*Si mangia!* It's time to eat!', everyone looked up. No one hesitated; they downed tools and strode or ran to where Bruna would set up breakfast under the pear tree.

With a tall tower of food balanced on her head she glided towards the field. She'd tied the tower together with the four corners of a tablecloth. Inside it was an enormous loaf of dark brown bread so dry and crusty it sounded like hollow wood if you knocked on it, a round of mild pecorino cheese, a sausage of salami and a dozen plums. After laying out the food, Bruna rose to go back to the house for baby Pasquale, wine and water. When she returned, Mario, Maria and Artemio sat with their backs against the tree trunk, while the younger children gathered in a circle around the tablecloth. After Artemio had made himself a thick *panino*, Bruna made up the children's.

Artemio was facing the road, so he was the first to see Poggio's manager, Giubbotto, saunter onto the dirt track, accompanied by the dogs sounding their alarm. Poggio's guard and third man (*terzo uomo*) followed him. They walked in a line, one behind the other, as though protecting the order of their rank. All three were employees of Poggio's owner, their jobs to oversee, guard and protect the farm and its produce.

'Giubbotto,' Artemio muttered under his breath, before whistling the dogs into silence.

'Dear God, the man must have been born sixth,' said Mario, referring to the belief that the sixth child is born with the sixth sense. None of them waved in greeting, but continued to eat in silence, waiting for the men to arrive.

Nicknamed Giubbotto (Jacket) because of his ridiculously dandy coats, Poggio's manager's real name was Giancarlo Mannucci. Thanks to their fabric shop in Stia, Giubbotto's parents had been able to afford to send their son to school till second grade. His mother, an overweight woman with eleven children, had had the good sense to apprentice her son into the farm management trade at ten years old, after promising to maintain a good discount on her goods to Poggio's owner's wife. Every *mezzadro* farm in Tuscany had a manager. Their work was to keep a livestock, seed and yield log, as well as accept and request payments for owners. Farmers had no contact with their masters; their managers interceded on all matters for them. Therefore, the managers had considerable power. Guards and third men protected against the theft of produce and tools.

After starting work as a third man, Giubbotto had worked his way up to farm guard, then to manager and now, at around twenty-three years old, could be regarded as successful because he managed five of Poggio's owner's twenty-seven farms. In the four years that Giubbotto had been making sure that the Brunis were meeting their dues and not thieving from his boss, he had arrived either on the day of scything or the day before. He knew his harvest days, Artemio gave him that.

The Brunis studied the men openly as they stalked towards them. Giubbotto, whose taste was highly questionable, was wearing a blue cotton jacket with linguini-thin red piping down the lapel and pockets, a faded rust-coloured shirt and brown trousers. Always he wore at his throat a small square of fabric, folded into a triangle and tied behind his neck, like a bandit ready to pull it up over his nose and rob a bank. Artemio suspected there was a bad rash lurking behind that kerchief.

When the men were about twenty metres away, Artemio poured himself a cup of wine, drank it down in one swift motion, then wiped his moustache with the back of his hand. He stood and made to walk around the tablecloth towards Giubbotto; as he did so he felt rather than heard Mario stand up too. Artemio didn't wait for his son, but walked forward to greet the manager.

'*Buon giorno*, Mr Farm Manager,' Artemio said without removing his hat.

'*Buon giorno*, Bruni,' replied Giubbotto. He had his hands in his pockets and made no move to remove them to shake hands, small signs from both men that they were ill at ease in each other's company. The guard and the third man stood away from them, their expressions distrustful, as though skeptical of finding honesty in any farmer. Their hard faces matched their strong bodies. They leant on the nearby orchard trees, listening to, but taking no part in, the conversation.

Giubbotto shifted slightly to his right, better to see Mario over Artemio's shoulder. 'Mario,' he nodded by way of recognition. Then he nodded to Bruna and slid his eyes slowly past Maria. Mario looked hard at him but did not move forward.

Giubbotto took his hands out of his pockets and, as was his habit, put one arm across his chest, thrust out his jaw and scratched his neck behind the scarf. Along with overseeing the collection of dues, the livestock's health, the condition of the farm tools and seeds and the harvesting of the grain and chestnuts, it was Giubbotto's job to tell the Brunis when they could commence threshing. Under no circumstances could a farmer thresh his grain without his manager and guards. The process had to be observed closely so that no one could steal a portion of the wheat. Farms could only thresh one at a time and Giubbotto had to be present.

'You should have it all in by dusk, no?'

As Artemio turned to look at the field he felt a breeze dry the sweat on his back. It smoothed the wheat tips like the caress of an invisible hand.

'Yes, we'll be ready by tomorrow.'

'Then you'll thresh tomorrow. Podervecchio started scything four days ago and finished yesterday. I'll tell the Podervecchio boys to come here tomorrow.'

Before Giubbotto there had been another manager, an old man beside whom Artemio had farmed for years. He had guided rather than governed Artemio for many of his early seasons at Poggio. But he had passed away and been replaced by Guibbotto, and Artemio could not help but think of him now. He would have offered the old man a glass of wine and had Bruna make him up a thick *panino*. They would have discussed the harvest, the other farms and the weather. When it was time to thresh, the former farm manager would have bashed the grain with the rest of them. Instead, Giubbotto lounged up against a tree, watching and waiting, as if hoping to catch someone stealing. No hospitality was possible with the new, young manager. Artemio felt sad that this was the case.

He agreed with Giubbotto's commands with a barely discernable inclination of his head. Giubbotto turned to his guard and pointed to the far side of the field. The man set out for it while Giubbotto indicated the barn door to the third man. Both would sit out the day at their watch posts, observing the Brunis' every move. The third man would be especially vigilant to make sure that no sheaves were being squirrelled away instead of being piled onto the haystack.

'Till then,' Artemio said and turned back to his family as Giubbotto walked off.

As they watched the retreating figures, Mario thrust forward his hips and began to scratch his neck vigorously in a rude imitation of their manager.

Maria stifled a laugh and Bruna held up her hand.

'That's enough,' she said softly.

4

By the time the shadows had stretched across the courtyard, Artemio was not sure where his movements began and ended. After sixteen hours of hard physical labour his body was slow, his mind several beats behind his actions. Perhaps that's why he started to shake when he saw Campo Alto's manager walk up Poggio's track. So much so, that in those first few seconds he was more surprised by his own trembling than by the manager's visit.

   The harvest was done and Poggio's guard and third man had only just left their positions, satisfied that the Brunis would not purloin any sheaves and that they could remember the exact height of the haystack even if they did. Artemio had been gathering up the sickles, pitchforks and other tools when he had glanced down the track and seen the approaching figure. While his mind searched for reasons for the visit, his heart knew exactly why Signor Certini had come. That's why he was shaking.

Even though it was almost dark he'd identified his brother's farm manager immediately – no man in Casentino was as small as Signor Certini. In the distance he appeared child-like, his round felt hat making him resemble a spindly brown mushroom. When he saw him hesitate in front of the barking dogs, Artemio called them off with a low growl. Slowly he turned to put his tools down against the wall of the house, using the time to collect his thoughts, but as he walked a little way down the track to greet his guest, his mind was still so befuddled he did not see a cloud of tiny insects and walked straight into it.

'Damn,' he muttered, spitting bugs and waving his hand back and forth in front of his face.

'*Buona sera*,' waved Signor Certini, his hat now in his hand.

'*Buona sera*, Signor Certini,' replied Artemio, picking a bug off his lip. As they came closer to each other, they both put their hands out to shake.

'I see you have it all in,' said Signor Certini, indicating as widely as he could with his little arms. 'Good, good,' he nodded approvingly, as though the farm were his to manage.

Artemio liked Signor Certini. He'd known him for years and they had talked often down at the bar in Stia where the men sat around tables drinking wine after their business was done at the weekly market. He was affable, with none of Giubbotto's arrogance. He'd grown up under the *mezzadria* farming system himself but had had the luck to fill in for a wealthy landowner's manager when he had fallen ill. The landowners found Certini was good at the job and learnt quickly, so they gave him three of their fifteen farms to manage. Certini had learnt to read and write at thirty years old and was now in his mid-sixties. He had Artemio's respect.

'I hear the chestnuts have treated you well at Poggio,' said Signor Certini, turning his back on Artemio to look up towards the wood beyond the road.

'Yes.' Artemio couldn't think of anything else to say.

'You've gained a reputation for having a special touch with them – it seems they grow for you.'

Artemio nodded cordially.

'Look, I won't make this a long story,' Certini said, his smile fading as he became serious. 'Campo Alto's not doing as well as it should under your brother's care.'

Artemio fixed his eyes on the field, razed to just below his knees. Signor Certini wasn't sure that Artemio had heard him until he nodded again.

'Sauro's down on his dues,' Certini went on. 'He's not managing, was even unable to deliver one of his Easter gifts to his owner. Cursed, I think.' He looked closely at Artemio, and then spat on the ground. 'Campo Alto's owner has heard of your work here and he wants you to take Sauro's farm. We feel you might be ready to leave your chestnuts.'

It was as Artemio thought. He was being offered his brother's farm.

'I'm sorry but you'll have to make your decision now. I've brought with me a standard contract cancellation for Poggio and one for Campo Alto. Sauro has already signed his. Tomorrow is 30 July. We have to have this done by the thirty-first.'

Artemio turned to look at the mountain which towered above his house. He thought of Campo Alto (High Field) nestled neatly along the top of it, just off the main Casentino thoroughfare. There'd be no more hauling his produce up and down the steep, rutted track that ran beside Poggio – the government cared for Campo Alto's road, filling its potholes regularly. It had two or three large fields. He could run more pigs, grow more grain.

Still, he was uncertain. The thought of living without chestnuts made him feel insecure. Living on a property with chestnuts was better than living on land with a gold seam. They were reliable and could be counted upon to feed his family when every other crop failed. His mother and father and their mothers and fathers had lived throughout winter on chestnut flour. It was all he knew. Mixed with water and cooked it became chestnut polenta. For breakfast the thick porridgy polenta was smothered in crunchy pieces of pork fat or mixed with pecorino cheese or jam. Bruna baked it into a sweet slice topped with sprigs of rosemary, pinenuts and sultanas. When the sleet and hail stole their winter vegetables she boiled dried chestnuts with water to make a smoky, satisfying soup. Every night they were roasted in pans as a supplement to dinner or a snack before bed. Artemio rubbed his chin and imagined life at Campo Alto.

The farm had ten extra hectares and thirty sheep, compared with his flock of fifteen. If managed well, a farm like Campo Alto could bring in a cash profit. Real money. With chestnuts, he farmed to survive. If he wanted to get ahead he would have to leave them to breed animals and produce cheese to sell. With that thought, a small seed took root in his mind. Ever since he was a small boy he'd wanted his own land. Who hadn't? But no matter how hard a *mezzadro* strove to pursue his dream, it was almost impossible to save enough cash to buy property. He had some small savings, money that Bruna had hidden away. He added to it when he could. But Poggio would not make money because it simply was not big enough. If he stayed on, relying solely on his chestnuts, he would never become his own landlord. This Campo Alto offer could be the opportunity of his life.

He made his decision and turned back to Signor Certini, who was waiting patiently for his answer.

'I'll take it,' he said calmly.

'Bravo, bravo,' Signor Certini said.

'Come inside. I'll sign now,' Artemio said. *'Non ti mettere in cammino se la bocca non sa di vino!* Don't leave unless your mouth tastes of wine!'

'Quite, quite,' said Signor Certini, smiling at the Casentino saying.

Inside the house it was pitch black, save for two candles that cast golden rings of light where Mario sat carving a prosciutto that had been hanging inside the fireplace, drying smooth and streaky. The fat was clear and the meat scarlet, its salty sharpness offset by the mild lard. Mario gripped it between his knees so as to cut it finely, his fingertips covered in peppery seasoning and pork oil. He carved it upwards in a semi-circular shape, so that when they reached the bone there would be plenty of meat left across the length of it.

Maria was also at the table, rubbing the pulp of mature tomatoes onto slices of bread. When the bread was soaked in juice, she put the slices onto a plate, drizzled oil across them, and then sprinkled the dish liberally with shredded basil and salt. Nine-year-old Silvio, clearly exhausted, sat with his elbows propping him up, never taking his half-closed eyes off the food being prepared. Anna was at the sink taking parsley leaves off their stems. Fiamma, Ottavia and baby Pasquale were already in bed.

Bruna stood at the end of the table crumbling a loaf of bread. When she saw Signor Certini walk into the kitchen behind Artemio, she started, a look of surprise on her face.

Then she wiped her hands on her apron and snapped into action.

'*Buona sera*, have you eaten? We had some minestrone earlier but will eat more now. Please join us.' Bruna did not know Signor Certini, and visitors on the eve of the harvest were rare. She addressed him formally, without a hint of curiosity. Certini responded in kind.

'*Buona sera* to you, Signora Bruni. You are most gracious, but I must return to my own wife, who very shortly will begin to think I've been eaten by wolves.'

'Fetch the wine, Bruna,' said Artemio, then added simply, 'We'll be taking on Campo Alto.'

'Well!' Bruna let escape.

The children stared at their parents, waiting to see who would speak first.

'Yes, I've come to ask Bruni to give up his chestnuts,' Certini said, smiling again, sensing the need to defuse a potentially uncomfortable situation.

'I mean,' Bruna went on, 'Sauro won't take to it, Artemio. He's your little brother.'

'That's not my concern,' Artemio replied sharply. 'It's a good farm. A better farm than this. Fetch the wine.' Artemio pulled out a seat for his guest. Bruna knew not to oppose her husband. He led the family, determined their future; what Bruna thought was of little consequence. She stayed quiet.

Signor Certini pulled one of the candles towards him and sat down on a wooden chair. He kept his bottom on the edge of his seat so that his feet did not swing in midair. Rummaging through his jacket pocket for his papers, ink and pen, he turned to his side and spat near his foot, inching even further off his chair to rub the gob of phlegm into the floorboards with the sole of his shoe. Artemio drew his chair up to the table and sat down beside him. Signor Certini laid out two pieces of paper. The Bruni family was dead quiet, their hands still at their chores, observing every move and word.

'You can take possession after 31 January 1907, but if your brother is willing, any time from now. If Sauro Bruni has not found lodgings by 31 January, he has one month's grace and you will have to hold off your move. If he is not out by 1 March 1907, the marshals will forcibly remove him. Any questions?'

Artemio was aware of this process, though only through hearsay. He squinted his eyes in concentration and nodded.

'Remember, you will sow here at Poggio and return to reap your last harvest of wheat, oats, barley, beans … whatever you have planted. It's yours and Poggio's owner's. Sauro, too. He will return to Campo Alto to reap what he sowed. After that, neither of you will return to your old farms.'

Signor Certini pointed to the Poggio contract and dipped his pen in ink before passing it to Artemio, whose hands looked like bear paws beside Signor Certini's. They were broad and brown, his fingers as thick as sausages. Etched into them were black cracks filled with dirt that in winter would split and bleed. He took the pen that Signor Certini offered him. Holding it awkwardly, he scrawled a large X on the dotted line.

'Good,' said Signor Certini, putting Poggio's contract aside to dry. 'Now, this is Campo Alto's – it's for fifteen years.'

Artemio smoothed it with his hands and peered at it closely, as though by looking at it hard enough he could make some sense of the letters. Eventually he added his X to that page too.

Signor Certini took the pen and neatly wrote his name as witness, then the date beside Artemio's X.

'Now it's time for that glass of wine, I think,' said Artemio's future manager while he turned once again to spit on the floor.

Bruna poured their wine and both men downed it, before pouring another. When they had drunk that, Signor Certini rose. He bid each member of the family goodnight, as though meeting them for the first time. He was happy; he had accomplished what he had set out to do.

Outside, the men shook hands. The breeze had quickened, as it did every evening after dark. It carried the smell of fresh hay and the sound of a night bird croaking throatily in the thicket down near the stream. The men turned and walked away from each other, Signor Certini briskly with his hat back on, Artemio slowly as he made his way thoughtfully towards his tools.

Back inside, Mario threw back his head and laughed. 'My cousins are going to be furious! Damn, I wish I'd been there when they were served their eviction orders. Oi oi!'

'But where will Uncle Sauro go? What will they do?' asked Maria.

'They'll move back in with Nonno and Nonna Bruni, that's what they'll do,' said Bruna. She was already resigned to the decision, and had vigorously taken up her bread grating for the goose's-neck stuffing, but she was nervous. Taking over Sauro's farm confused her. She wanted it, wanted the extra money the sheep's cheese would bring, the respect that running a bigger, better farm would command, but she knew it would distance the Bruni brothers even further. The two men had never been close and had not seen each other for years. Too many sad, hungry and difficult times during their childhood had eaten away at what could have been a warm relationship. Bruna often thought about visiting Sauro and his wife, but although they'd never talked about it, she'd gleaned that Artemio would not approve of her socialising with them. He would think it disloyal, as though she were betraying his wishes.

'We could take Nonno and Nonna Bruni with us to Campo Alto, no?' asked Maria.

Bruna's face was shadowy in the dim light. Maria did not need to see her mother's expression to know that she was thinking hard. Her grating slowed, then she ran her fingers inattentively through the breadcrumbs, distantly thumbing the crust into powder.

'What do you think?' Maria insisted.

'I think you have a good idea,' said Bruna. She knew then that they would take Artemio's parents to live with them at Campo Alto and that Sauro would take the room at Omomorto on his own. In this, she would have her say.

'Toh! Wonderful!' Mario roared mirthfully. 'We'll take our cousins' farm and their grandparents too. Oh, this is too good!'

Silvio, having eaten his fill, leant over and spat on the floor by his foot.

In one swift stride, Bruna was beside him. She swatted him soundly over the back of his head with her open hand. 'Don't even *think* about developing that disgusting habit.'

That was the night the Brunis' lives began to change.

5

August
Poggio's Forest

By the end of August, Tuscany's grain, barley and oat harvest was over. The sheep, no longer being milked for ricotta and pecorino, rested in the shade. The chickens scratched in the heat, laying their eggs every other day rather than every day. The apples and pears bided their time, waiting to be picked and packed away in the larder, along with the odd pot of blackberry and strawberry jam. Only a few of the figs had yet matured. They dried on trays balanced on rocks in the garden, while the garlic bulbs and onions lost their moisture hanging in brown, scraggly bunches above the doorways and porches.

In the mountains around the town of Stia, the news of Artemio's surprise Campo Alto offer had spread and the district now accepted his move as fact. Giubbotto had received Poggio's contract cancellation and another family was being sought to take the Brunis' place.

It was on one of these last hot summer mornings, before the sun began to wane towards autumn and the rains came, that Artemio took Mario to the chestnut trees. They had to clear the forest floor in preparation for when the chestnuts ripened and dropped to the ground. They swung in their hands hatchets, rakes, wooden stakes and hammers, while their feet fell into the rhythm of the chiming cuckoo birds. 'Cuckoo! Cuckoo!' called one for five minutes till another one picked up the beat as though passing along a birdsong baton. The woods were full of them, along with birds that cried like babies and others that hummed by so close they sounded like cats purring.

Under the foliage it was dark and cool, the sunshine above speckling its light on the composting leaves below. The air smelt of wet earth and there was moss on the rocks. Every now and then the branches screeked out a whine as the wind pushed through them. Artemio noticed with satisfaction that the green ceiling was a galaxy of prickly chestnut casings.

In silence the men set to raking hard so that there would be no rotten leaves to hamper their harvest. They were careful not to damage the trunks or scrape any roots as they tugged at the weeds and shrubs. Fallen twigs and branches were dragged into the sun to dry and be carried home for kindling. Some of the soil was turned to give the plants what Artemio thought was the greatest fertiliser of all: oxygen.

When done, Artemio felt that his trees could now breathe and he, too, inhaled deeply. Then he began to move through the woods from chestnut to chestnut. With his head bowed he placed his hand on each trunk, murmuring softly. He felt deeply indebted to these trees and believed without a doubt that each one had its own personality. Some, as tall as a church's steeple with intertwining trunks, were like loyal old friends. They were more than eighty years old and would in several months generously present him with around two hundred and fifty kilos of chestnuts. He felt fortunate in their kindness. The middle-aged chestnuts gave well too, but like people reluctant to leave their youth behind, they had not yet reached their full potential. The adolescent ones, their leaves shiny and red with immaturity, still had to prove themselves, although one day, Artemio was confident, they would be as giving as their grandfathers. Artemio rested his forehead against the craggy bark of a cloud-shaped chestnut and thought about the bad seeds. Selfishly, they yielded nothing and took all the goodness from the givers nearby. He hacked the takers down, to maintain the group's harmony.

He could hear Mario hammering stakes in behind small barricade logs. They would catch the runaway chestnuts where the ground sloped.

'Mario!' he called. 'Have you had a good look at them yet?'

Artemio heard his son back away from his work to join him. They looked into the first layer of iridescent, spiky green pompoms, to the next layer and the layer after that and realised that this year there were masses of chestnuts. More than ever before.

'Well, would you look at that,' Mario muttered, craning to see further into the higher branches. 'We'll never gather this lot on our own.'

Artemio grunted thoughtfully.

Within a week he was on his way down to Stia to hire two hands to help bring in the chestnuts. It was the first time he had employed anyone.

⁂

The town of Stia had been given its name five hundred years before by a policeman who apprehended two highwaymen.

At the time the town was called Staggia, after the creek that ran by its side. The bandits camped in the nearby forest, wearing pants and shirts made from the hides of animals they had trapped and skinned; their filthy hair and grisly beards reached down to their waists, where daggers and hooks jangled as they walked. These men made their living from ambushing travellers on the road to Florence. The famous policeman lay in wait and caught them, but instead of jailing them, he made them an offer. 'If you can bring a rock down from the Falterona, you can go free.' The thieves then climbed Falterona Mountain – the king of all the Casentino peaks, at 1650 metres high – and for the next three days and nights dragged a rock down its side. When the policeman was satisfied with the position of the rock he said, '*Basta che stia lì.* It can stay there.' Stia means 'stay' and so the name stayed as well as the rock.

Over the next five hundred years the town flourished. The Staggia creek joins the Arno creek at Stia, to create one coursing river that skips its way down to Florence, then on to quench much of Tuscany's thirst. Stia's walls were eventually fortified against the river's angry winter rush. In time, the people harnessed the water's power to fuel the growing demand for steel, wool and leather. Stia's mills and textile-dyeing factories prospered and became highly regarded in Europe. Its wool was unique, a thick weave with hardy nubs that became its trademark. By the early 1900s the town's population had swelled to several thousand people, five hundred of whom worked exclusively for the mills. Many of the workers were women so, compared with the rest of Italy, Stia held emancipated views. Homes, schools and a theatre sprouted to house, educate and entertain the mill families, making the town one of the most dynamic in rural Tuscany, with a thriving *borghese* (middle class).

Stia's piazza was surrounded by four-storey palazzos, all painted in varying hues of sandy beige. Each storey had two or three square windows protected by solid green shutters. Under each palazzo were medieval square or contemporary arched porticoes, depending on which century they had been added to the piazza. Behind the porticoes' columns were millers; shoe shops; a cobbler; a book, pen and ink merchant; and a tool shop that sold lamps, candles, axe heads and handles.

The town's market had for centuries been held on a Tuesday, drawing in the surrounding farmers. They sold their produce, bartered for livestock, found out the current value of their animals or met with their farm's manager. Clonking into the piazza, wearing their three-inch wooden soles, the rural men were not difficult to sort from the town's folk. The men of the land wore simple clothes that had been sewn from hemp at home; their shirts had no collars and were open, often with a rolled kerchief around their neck. Most wore their best jackets, and when they took them off they rolled up their sleeves and secured their shirts into their pants by winding long strips of material around their waists. They did not like belts. They said they restricted their movements and dug into their stomachs.

The farmers also distinguished themselves by their odd walk, a sort of slide and lurch as though they were skating on black ice, which, in fact, they almost were. Under their wooden soles were *bullette*, dozens of thick iron nails. These tacks worked a dream on the dirt roads – they gripped the stones and mud like exaggerated football boots. But *bullette* on cobblestones were another matter entirely. They had no purchase on the smooth, black stones and often made the farmers fall.

The *sensale* Artemio went to see at the top of the piazza looked smart in his fashionable cotton suit that one of the best tailors in Stia had sewn. His boots were of fine leather.

'*Guarda chi c'è!* Look who is here!' called the *sensale* when he saw Artemio scrabbling his way up the cobblestones. When not moving among the livestock or out visiting farms, the *sensale*'s office was a chair and table outside the café at the top end of the steep, teardrop-shaped piazza.

'*Buon giorno*, Signor Sensale,' panted Artemio. 'I have need of your services for November.'

'Do you now?' The *sensale* raised his considerable eyebrows, endowed thickly upon his plump face and matched by the tufts of hair that crowded his nostrils. 'The Bruni touch with chestnuts, I presume?'

Artemio was surprised and wondered how he knew of his harvest and whether the *sensale* was making fun of him. Till now there had been no business between them.

'Your reputation precedes you.' The *sensale* laughed as he turned Artemio towards his table and chair, patting him on the back.

As the livestock broker for the mountainous regions of Casentino, Stia's *sensale* made it his business to know everyone's business. He had informants up and down even the most remote tracks. They reported to him on the births and deaths of animals (babies' births did not concern him), sick sows or diseased cows. The farmers also brought him presents. A chicken, a bag of beans, a salami or a prosciutto, olive oil, wine. Whatever they could afford. It was essential to have the *sensale* on your side. Without him, there was no sale or purchase of your animals. He was the man legally appointed to set the price for your beast before it was taken to market. He also brokered the tools, seeds and animals when a farm changed hands. The estimation of the value of everything that kept a farmer alive fell to him. Often called the 'estimator', the *sensale* was the cornerstone of all farming arrangements. And he answered to no higher authority. His word was law.

As Artemio sat down, he gingerly put a bag of carefully wrapped eggs on the table.

'You'll be moving to Campo Alto too, I'm told. *Un bel podere!* A fine farm! You'll do well there. I'll come to Campo Alto to sort out the goods later, when you're ready to take the chestnuts to the mill. Leave it till November, eh?' As he spoke he opened Artemio's gift and peered inside the bag. Saying nothing, he put the eggs on the chair beside him. Artemio noticed there were other hessian sacks there too.

'It is about the chestnuts, Signor Sensale. I have many this year and will need help collecting and drying them.'

'I have some women from Emilia Romagna. Good women. I'll send word. You can collect them on the second market day of October.'

'Two, all right?' Artemio felt proud, if somewhat nervous, making these arrangements. He needed to speak of the workers' wages and accommodation but felt unsure of how to do that. As he opened his mouth to speak, a voice bellowed behind him.

'It's Littlelegs talking to the *sensale*. What could Littlelegs possibly be wanting with the *sensale*?'

'Claudio! *Buon giorno*,' greeted the *sensale*. 'Come, Claudio, sit. We need a witness for this deal.' He waved the man onto the chair next to Artemio, while Artemio pulled his chair as far away from the table as possible, cringing at his close proximity.

'A pleasure. A pleasure,' replied the man, whose hair was

as red as the rash of broken capillaries that spidered his face. 'Anything for my neighbour, eh?' He winked at Artemio's discomfort and smiled. His lips were fleshy and wet. They hid a mouth overcrowded with stained, black teeth.

Nicknamed Il Rosso (the Red), the proposed witness lived at Il Villaggio, a few kilometres up the road from Poggio, his house across the road from Artemio's church. The two men's lower fields were separated only by a thicket so they saw each other often, though never greeted each other. Both were farmers, both worked twenty hectares of land, but between the two there was one big difference and Il Rosso never let Artemio forget it. Il Rosso *owned* his land, and that, on the ladder of Tuscan country life, made Il Rosso one rung above Artemio.

'Artemio here needs two women for his chestnuts,' said the *sensale*.

'Aya! You've a good haul! You'll be eating them all winter. What good fortune!' Il Rosso's last observation was thick with sarcasm.

'We'll be eating more than chestnuts this year,' Artemio measured his reply evenly. He folded his arms and looked at the tabletop, refusing to take Il Rosso's bait.

'Just food and board for the women?' went on the *sensale*. 'I'd also recommend ten kilos of chestnuts each. Helps them move faster.'

'*Si*, Signor Sensale, that sounds fair,' responded Artemio.

'That's it then: two women from Emilia Romagna. They receive food and board and ten per cent of what they gather. And a *staio* [a wooden container that holds eighteen kilos] of chestnuts for me.' The *sensale* held his hand out across the table. Artemio took it and they shook vigorously three times. Then Il Rosso raised his hand above theirs and, in a movement like a sharp karate chop, brought it down over the men's hands. In the illiterate world of farmers, this three-handed shake was the contract. With Il Rosso the witness, the deal was done.

Back at Poggio, Bruna was nearing the house after being out since before sunrise collecting *nipitella*, the small furry herb that grew wild in the fields. It had a faint aroma of tobacco and she wanted to add it to the first mushrooms of the season. Unlike *porcini*, the summer mushrooms did not grow in the forest. They liked the sunshine in the open fields, and this morning she'd had a feeling that they would have sprouted beside the road and on the common behind the church. Her hunch proved correct and she now had quite a collection. She would fry them up with the *nipitella* and garlic. Bruna had also found some *salvastrella* to add to her bean soup. The tiny leaves looked like parsley but smelt like cucumber, so made the soup taste fresh and light. Tucked into her apron were several fistfuls of *mesticanza*, wild field grass. The long, thick, bittersweet blades would be tossed with oil, vinegar, salt and tomatoes for lunch. On her back and tied with a string was a huge bundle of grass for her rabbits. It had been a good morning, a morning that would feed her family well.

The two dogs, catching her scent before she turned onto Poggio's track, announced her arrival with whimpers and whines. As she approached the house they greeted her with half-crawl humility.

'And you would abandon your sheep?' she said to them affectionately. '*Via, via.* Go, go.' Unwillingly, the dogs slunk back to their station by the pen.

Several metres from the front door, Bruna heard shrill, angry screams from her daughters. She did not need to make out the words to know what their fight was about. Anger and frustration tightened in her chest. Ottavia would have wet the bed again and, once more, the girls would reek of her stale urine. By the day's end the stink of it would permeate the house. The yellow-stained sheets and the soaked cornhusks would have to hang from the windows to dry. She untied the rabbits' grass, hurled it onto the ground by the door and walked inside.

'Ottavia!' yelled Bruna up the stairs.

The girls' fighting stopped abruptly.

'*Si, mamma,*' came a small voice from the bedroom.

'*Ora tu ne buschi.* Now you're going to get it.' Bruna heard Fiamma's whisper. She could also hear baby Pasquale wailing. He was stuck in bed, bound tight.

'Fiamma! Bring your brother downstairs and change him. Now!'

Fiamma huffed in complaint to Maria, who was already coming down the stairs.

Mario's and Silvio's stomps came overhead as they readied themselves for the day, and Bruna moved towards the shelves for the bread. Maria would set the table and go to the garden to retrieve the *baccelli* (beans in their pods) and onions for breakfast. Anna would go to the stream for the morning's water.

By the time Bruna turned around, Ottavia stood at the bottom of the stairs with a runny nose and a quivering bottom lip. It inspired no sympathy in her mother. With two long steps she was upon her. She slapped her mercilessly with an open hand on the girl's shoulders, cheeks and head.

'You piss in your bed one more time and your father will do the beating,' she hissed.

Ottavia nodded quickly.

'You're four years old. No more bed-wetting!' When she stepped away from the little girl, Bruna was breathing heavily. She had never before hit Ottavia. But there seemed to be no other way to teach the child to stop her filthy, shameful habit. Already the acrid smell of urine was in the kitchen. It made Bruna nauseous. Spinning around she told Anna to change Ottavia's clothes and wash them in the stream after breakfast.

'Silvio, cut and stack the wood and put it by the oven. Fiamma, that ewe with the new lamb, she has an infection in her teat; separate her from her lamb today. Anna, when you come back from the woods with the pigs, help Fiamma feed the lamb with another ewe's milk. If you're not strong enough, call Mario. Maria, get the last of the ripe tomatoes and put them with the others and prepare them for the tomato sauce. Mario, finish the new potatoes today. Ottavia, you will feed the chickens, tend to the eggs, then stay in your room by your mattress until it's dry.'

All the while Bruna's hands never stopped moving. After some minutes, tears filled her eyes so that the bread she was slicing appeared to ripple in liquid. She slipped onto the floor and covered her face with her hands. Her remorse made her feel sick.

'Come here, baby,' she called to Ottavia. Her littlest girl came to her, her chin puckered as she tried to control her grief. Bruna held out her arms and folded her child inside them. She squeezed her close, put her nose into Ottavia's hair and let her lips touch its baby softness.

'I'm sorry, my love. I'm sorry.' Sitting there on the kitchen floor, with Ottavia curled on her lap, it felt as if her bones were so weary they were melting through the floorboards. 'There's just too much to do without you adding your pee pee to it all.' She rested her head back against the cupboard door and closed her eyes. *Just another minute to sit, like this, please,* she thought.

***

It is said that the men of rural Tuscany fell into two categories: those who teased and those who took it. The jokers were the ones who managed to do their work in the fields while telling funny stories or singing silly verses. They would husk the corn with banter, playing the wag till everyone laughed. If someone had a sore point, these jokers would find it, and if sensitivity was shown, the laughs only came harder. Consequently the Tuscans are famous for their leg-pulling and practical jokes. The teasing was born, quite literally, from there being nothing else to do. Taking the mickey was free and few took offence because, most of the time, the jokes fell short of cruel mocking. It was done to lighten the mood, and therefore the workload. Everyone believed you were either a born comic, or not. If not, you were needled. The teased took the wisecracks because the alternative, being a social outcast, was far worse. It was better to be ridiculed in fun and among people than to pout in a corner alone.

When he was younger, Artemio Bruni had possessed a dry irony that people enjoyed. They thought he was clever. But that was gone now. He had run out of patience with the jokers and their monkey tricks. He felt that the funny men were weak, less determined than the strong men, and that they compensated for their lack of strength with humour. They couldn't pull stumps but could carry on effortless conversations. Their words slipped easily from their tongues, like their work through their fingers. With this irritability Artemio had begun to show his age, which, at forty-four, in the Tuscan mountains of 1906, was old. The wags could afford to joke because they had not yet paid the price of years of solitude and relentlessly hard labour. Life had ground most men Artemio's age into silence. They had lost sons whom they would never forget but rarely had time to remember.

Pranksters, chatterboxes or crankily stern, whatever their character it made no difference to the farmers who came into town on Tuesdays, for each one wrapped himself in a cloak of silence. In the piazza, everybody shrank from the offensive behaviour of the city slickers.

One farmer, known among his friends for having the best baritone at *veglia*, had never uttered a word in town. He shuffled in, with his head down, and, when asked, pointed towards the place he was heading. Until one day he caught his foot under a loaded cart. When he yelled out a series of expletives, the nearby shopkeepers were stunned and called, 'My God! We thought that man was mute!'

It wasn't Stia's bustling activity or the feeling of being confined by the tall buildings that made the men withdraw into themselves. Nor was it the noise or the pervasive smells coming from the dye vats and steelworks. The farmers changed when they came to town because the townspeople hated them.

For generations the city dwellers had dismissed the country people as ignorant and treated them with disdain. The contempt started early, as the urban children knew the rural children were illiterate. So, dressed in their sailor suits or knickerbockers with leather boots and long socks, the city children tormented the farm boys, tricking them into falls, such as when a trio of them teased a young shepherd about his ratty jacket. They said it was good for nothing and when the boy turned his back, they put it under a mule to catch its falling dung. The young shepherd's parents were too unsure of themselves to talk to the trio's parents. They simply retreated further into themselves and kept even more to their own folk.

To avoid standing out in any way, the farmers stuck together in groups of five or ten, leaning against the walls of the piazza, talking quietly while watching their livestock or rounds of cheese. If a farmer was noticed, he risked derision and sarcasm. In fear of the sneers and town con tricks, the men from the land kept to themselves and had nothing at all to do with the bourgeois society of Stia.

Artemio, on the way to his usual café, responded meekly to town animosity. He was a brave man in the forest, had once fought a pack of wolves with his back up against a tree – beat them off with sheer anger and a swinging sickle – but in the face of Stia's scorn, he felt lost.

With his head down, mouth pursed into a grim line and his shoulders back, Artemio opened the café's door. Once inside, the smell of black pepper pricked at his nostrils, making him want to rub his nose. The pungent, pinelike pepper was sold in barrels and used to cover the prosciuttos that hung from the ceiling. As if wanting to direct customers towards the counter, the floor space was lined with open sacks of rice, lentils, polenta, barley, chickpeas and four different types of beans – Toscanelli, cannellini, San Matteo and borlotti. Brooms and wooden crates of powdered detergents crowded what little space was left.

As his eyes adjusted to the darkness, the first person Artemio saw was Giubbotto. He was hard to miss in a mustard-yellow cotton jacket and trousers.

'*Buon giorno*, Mr Farm Manager,' said Artemio sombrely.

'*Buon giorno*, Bruni. I have found a family for Poggio!' Giubbotto responded with satisfaction. He was at a table with one of his brothers. Not only were they similar in appearance, they clearly had the same taste in clothes. The man wore a suit identical to Giubbotto's, only his had navy buttons rather than brown. He nodded absently at Artemio as Giubbotto continued.

'He will be an asset to Poggio's owner, as he has many sons. I will bring him and the *sensale* up to Poggio after the chestnuts. You must tell me when you are vacating.' Giubbotto looked at Artemio expectantly.

'I will leave on 1 February, Mr Farm Manager.'

'No earlier?' Giubbotto looked puzzled.

'No.'

Giubbotto nodded, then resumed his conversation with his brother.

Artemio turned towards the counter and asked for three boxes of matches. The shopkeeper put them down beside a large set of scales. Behind him, beside some faded sepia postcards of Florence that hung crookedly from nails, was a long, low cupboard filled with dozens of small drawers. Inside were pastas shaped liked tiny halos, called Ave Marias (Hail Marys). Next to them were bigger halos, Paternostri (Our Fathers) and *stortini* (little crookeds), little hollow spaghetti pieces, penne, *stelline* and *risoni* – all sold by weight. There were large vats of Marsala, vin santo, olive oil and red and white wine. Tins of cloves, aniseed, vanilla and cinnamon lined the shelves next to glass jars of sugar and cocoa. Brown paper bags with their sides rolled down held almonds, hazelnuts, walnuts, pinenuts and pistachios. All products for sale to the town's residents. The Brunis ate what they either made or grew. Once in a while Artemio would buy salted fish and today he considered purchasing some salted cod – *baccala* – or smoked herring. Bruna would flour and fry the cod with garlic, tomatoes and potatoes. The smoked herring his family would rub onto bread slices or swipe along their toasted polenta. After virtually eating the odour of the herring for weeks, Bruna would ultimately slice it thinly and toss it with vinegar, oil and parsley as an antipasto on bread. Artemio decided on the herring because it lasted longer. He ordered it prepared before moving aside.

'Gambine, would you not join us?' called Marcello Mazzetti, Artemio's neighbour and Signora Mazzetti's husband. He was sitting at the back of the shop with Botte (Punches) under a sign that read: *Religion, good sense and civility forbid the use of vile language and blasphemy*.

'Ohhh ... Signor Mazzetti,' Artemio greeted, making his salutation long and musical to show that he was pleased to see his friend. '*Buon giorno!* I didn't see you there ... and Botte.'

Signor Marcello Mazzetti's eyes creased from a smile that was set in almost translucent skin. His hair, too, had become almost invisible, wispy and white as though the years were bleaching him of colour. His grin revealed one remaining canine, which poked out of his bottom jaw like a yellow corn kernel. While the rest of his teeth had fallen out when he was relatively young, this tooth stuck like a pebble in concrete and had caused Signor Mazzetti no end of discomfort. It had also given him his nickname, Dentino (Littletooth), because as far back as anyone could remember he'd only ever had this one tooth. Over the last few years people had stopped calling him Dentino, out of respect for his age. The slow cessation of his nickname marked an increase in the use of *voi*, the formal form of address reserved for the elderly and people of a higher station.

'You're well, I hope,' said Artemio, pulling up a seat.

'I am, though I fear my weekly trips to the market are numbered. It's my hips. And your bread trees?' he inquired, using Casentino's nickname for its chestnuts.

'Good enough for two extra hands this year,' said Artemio.

'Bravo! If you're expecting a good harvest, we'll have one too.' Signor Mazzetti rubbed his palms up and down his thighs as though they had become sweaty at the thought of all those fat chestnuts. He spoke like most people without teeth, his V's became B's, his F's became P's and his S's were a whistle that lasted long after the word was finished. 'Poggio's trees will miss you, as we will.'

Artemio bowed his head modestly at Signor Mazzetti's compliment, then addressed his other friend. 'Your cellar shining like silver, Botte?' asked Artemio, referring to the September preparations for the wine harvest. Those who had grapes were cleaning out their cellars, readying their barrels and flasks with much rinsing and wicker repairs.

'My weaver's coming this very afternoon. Can I keep aside a twenty-litre flask for you?' smiled Botte.

'Certainly, though there's no guarantee I'll buy it. Let's see how your grapes are this year – better than last, I hope. And you, Signor Mazzetti? Much toothache these days?'

'You have no idea. My wife's poppyseed tea is wonderful, though. Helps me sleep.'

'The time has come to see the blacksmith, surely?'

'No, no, no, we'll try again at home,' he said, shaking his head. Artemio had tried several times to pull Signor Mazzetti's tooth, but to no avail. The old man would not let him use anything that looked remotely like a wrench. He feared them more than the pain, though it was the only tool likely to work.

The conversation had moved on when a group of men entered the bar. All confident landowners, they noisily dragged their seats up to a table to share.

'Gambine!' a voice roared above the others, silencing the din. When Artemio looked over he saw Il Rosso standing rigid and serious, with his hand held out. The redhead lowered his palm quickly in a chopping movement. Contract witnesses were required to remind people of their deals on the day the deal was done. The public chop was to alert others to the agreement. Artemio nodded in acknowledgement while his friends stared. They now knew that Il Rosso was the witness to a recent transaction with Artemio.

'Ahem.' Botte cleared his throat. 'Got yourself a trustworthy witness there,' he mumbled sarcastically.

'*Sensale*'s choice, not mine,' Artemio muttered back. As he rose to take his leave and pay for his package, Signor Mazzetti touched his jacket.

'One moment. Come to *veglia* tonight. And bring the little one, Ottavia. My wife's fallen in love with that one. She's due for some young company. Could you spare her a night or two?'

Artemio smiled at Signor Mazzetti's request. When they were smaller, Silvio, Fiamma and Anna had often slept the night at the Mazzettis' house. The Bruni children helped the Mazzettis with their animals and did the jobs that required little hands and small bodies. It would be Ottavia's first night away from home. *Good practice for her*, Artemio thought. A comfortable beginning to sleeping in another person's house, something that all his daughters did and would do more and more as they grew older. Anna and Fiamma had both been sent into domestic service as maids at the larger farms, either to help with their harvest or to assist with the washing. Fiamma at six years old had spent an entire summer looking after a wealthy family's gaggle of geese, all done in return for food and board. For the Brunis it was one less mouth to feed and sometimes their children came home with a bag of grain or a set of matching buttons. Artemio could see no reason why he should refuse the Mazzettis' invitation.

'Bruna and I will see you tonight with Ottavia then.' Artemio pushed through the shop's door without looking at Il Rosso.

Back out in the sunshine, he looked across the piazza and adjusted his hat low over his eyes. The morning air was warm, laced with the smell of manure and vegetables lying in the sun. Men's voices ricocheted from wall to wall. 'Whoop, whoop' and 'Yip, yip' they called to their oxen as they guided them towards the main road and home. Goats, sheep and lambs were tethered in rows, the odd bag of hay separating them from each other. Unharnessed carts rested diagonally on the ground, their shafts sticking up, like ditched wheelbarrows. The farmers stacked crates of unsold spinach and turnips, their green plumes wilting in the heat. They moved around makeshift wooden benches that held small pyramids of zucchinis and tomatoes as well as piles of potatoes, packing them away into wicker baskets.

Three-quarters of the way up the piazza was a stone drinking fountain with four waist-high troughs around it. Each trough had a metre-long iron tap like a snake slithering out of a lion's mouth. Artemio paused by one, cupped his hand and drank deeply before his long walk home.

The track he paced was behind Stia and followed the stream right up to Poggio. It was wide enough for a donkey loaded on both flanks with baskets, but barely big enough to handle the oxen and carts that plied it with their heavy loads. To negotiate the ruts Artemio had to keep his head down and his eyes on the road. He took no notice of the wide, open fields dotted with olive trees pruned like chandeliers. The higher he rose the less the land was cleared, the altitude too high for the production of wine and olives, and soon the mountains became dense with trees.

Once he was past Campolombardo a wind sprang up. Artemio dipped his hat and averted his eyes as the dust clouded off the track. He angled his face towards the bushes beside the track and noticed as he did so a young elder tree. Slender and long, it made Artemio stop midstride. Quickly he walked towards it and pushed it to the ground, snapping it just above the soil. Glancing over his shoulder in case someone should see him, he put the trunk down and squatted to brush dirt, leaves and anything else he could find over the jagged stump to hide it. The trees on state land belonged to the government, and permission to cut them had to be sought from the forest guards. If he were caught stealing this elder there would be serious consequences. At best, he would receive an impossible fine; at worst, he would be thrown off his farm.

A man's whistle from perhaps five kilometres away pirouetted up to him on the wind. But with sound carrying so clearly from mountain to mountain, it was hard to judge the whistler's distance. Tucking the elder tree under his arm, Artemio continued briskly on his way. When he arrived home he went straight to the cheese room and hid his find under the shelves. He would pull it out again one night this winter and make the children new shoes with it.

6

The literal translation of the word *veglia* is 'to stay awake' or 'to sit up late', though throughout Italian history it has had a far deeper meaning. 'To gather in the company and security of good friends after darkness closes in' is a much better description of the warm-hearted camaraderie that emanates from a house holding *veglia*.

In the northern parts of rural Italy, several families often shared one enormous farmhouse that was divided into many homes. The families became friends and at night the men, women and children gathered in the barns or stables. They crammed together in the hay, staying close to their animals for warmth. One at a time, or all together, they sang funny or traditional songs and said their prayers.

In Casentino, the practice of many families sharing one building was not so common. Farmers had their own homes and they made friends with the people who lived up the road or worked the land nearby. Everyone took informal turns to host *veglia*, issuing the invitations with a wave and a yell from a passing cart or from across a field. '*Veglia! Stasera, da noi! Veglia!* Tonight at our house!' Friends would know then that after dinner, when the animals and children had been cared for, doors were open for visitors.

These Tuscan gatherings were held around the yawning warmth of the mammoth kitchen fireplaces. On average the hearths measured two metres by two metres, some raised only a few centimetres from the floor so that they looked like separate little fire rooms. Guests and hosts sat before the hearths according to age and honour, bestowed in silent acknowledgement of the day's work. The old and frail, with shawls across their shoulders and their feet wrapped in soft woollen socks and loosely laced boots, were closest to the flames, right inside the hearth on benches next to the grate. In front were breastfeeding mothers, exhausted fathers, uncles and other males, then aunties and friends. Last in line were the children, who squished in wherever they could alongside the group or behind it. They rubbed their exposed bottoms and arms, rotating their small bodies around and around like pork on spits to keep warm, as the air beyond the wall of people was frigid.

During *veglia* the elderly taught the young their stories and passed on their family histories. As the fire hummed, the families exchanged gossip, news and jokes while roasting chestnuts or cracking walnuts. On occasion, wine was enjoyed, but for the poorer, higher altitude families *vino* had to be purchased, or bartered, so they did not imbibe freely or regularly.

When not ruminating about agriculture, the men often played cards, grinning or groaning over games such as *scopa* (sweep), *briscola* (a points game with pictures of swords, cups and queens) and *uomo nero* (black man – the player left with the black Jack lost). The women never played games, preferring instead to sit separately and talk about food, the health of their families or remedies and cures for illnesses. A good woman managed to have food on her table. In this they upheld each other, gratefully sharing tips and advice. They disdained idle hands so kept their fingers busy with spinning wool or hemp, something they did by touch as there was not enough light to darn or embroider unless one brought one's own lamp.

Before setting off to *veglia* at the Mazzettis', Bruna called Maria upstairs to prepare Ottavia, telling her to wash her little sister's face and braid her hair. People did not dress up for these visits but stayed in their work clothes, so there was no need to change her dress. On the way out of the girl's bedroom, Bruna paused to put both hands on Ottavia's shoulders. She bent down and looked Ottavia in the eyes.

'You will not disgrace us tonight,' she said sternly. 'You will refuse any water offered and will not do pee pee in Signora Mazzetti's bed.' She softened her tone a little and hugged Ottavia. 'I know you will make us proud.' Then Bruna went to breastfeed and wrap baby Pasquale, finally putting him to sleep with Silvio, who had strict instructions to make sure the baby didn't roll off the bed.

Artemio, Bruna and Ottavia left their home under a dusk horizon streaked with orange, pink and purple. In the distance the castles of Porena, Poppi and Porciano appeared enormous. Majestically they lorded it over Stia's mill sheds and factories, which lay in a jumble of red oblongs at their feet. Bruna fell into step beside Artemio and drew her shawl close around her shoulders. A stag barked from the brook below the house, calling his mate, who moved slowly because of the baby deer at her side. Bruna knew that deer family well. They came every morning to her house, just as she and the sun rose for the day. The stag led his family to her lilies to eat the succulent leaves, shearing them down to the roots.

Three steps behind her parents followed Ottavia, the distance growing greater with each foot fall. Meandering in her thoughts, she could not help but feel favoured to be sleeping at the Mazzettis'. Secretly Ottavia hoped Signora Mazzetti would teach her a magic cant or even a spell, though she thought a big slice of jam tart was more likely and that was fine too. The excitement of it all made her want to be extra helpful with everything she did at the Mazzettis', intentions that would have come as no surprise to Bruna, as Ottavia tended to be a most diligent girl. She was eager to please in all her chores, though, as a result, exceedingly slow. Because of this, Bruna found that of all her children Ottavia most tried her patience. She found herself calling, 'Oh, hurry *up*, Ottavia!' frequently to her youngest daughter and it made her testy.

But still, Bruna had to concede that the child scampered off to do her jobs every morning without needing to be asked. She checked the chickens, putting her little finger expertly up inside a hen to check the progress of an egg that for some reason had not been laid. Then she tiptoed into the coop to collect the eggs, her face serious. She would put her finds into her basket with such precision that Bruna's breast swelled with tenderness.

Ottavia's instinctive caution convinced Bruna that the child was ready to have her responsibilities increased in spring when she turned five. To celebrate her birthday she would be given full charge of the sheep. From then on, Ottavia would spend her days watching over the flock, grazing them on the hillsides. Straight after breakfast she would arm herself with a stick bigger than she was, take a slab of bread, a chunk of cheese and a square of brown wax paper (this she would roll into a cone and drink from at the stream) and shepherd the sheep till late afternoon. At night she would help milk them and learn how to make ricotta and pecorino cheese. For her tenth birthday, just like her sisters before her, Ottavia would graduate onto the care of the pigs. Those she would take daily to the woods and stream to snout about for roots and acorns. Essentially, she would spend the next ten years of her life alone with the family's animals. Bruna was confident Ottavia would risk her life rather than see them stray. *As she should*, Bruna thought. Every future farmer's wife should love her animals as much as she loved her family. When Bruna glanced behind her to check on Ottavia's progress she saw that 'the little one', as she was dubbed by the Mazzettis, was away with the pixies.

'Oh, come *on*, Ottavia,' Bruna called. Artemio strode ahead, his boots crunching noisily along the gravel, his hands plunged deep into his pockets, but Bruna slowed her pace. The grassy green strip beside the road was speckled with white daisies and buttercup-yellow flowers shaped like gramophones. Ottavia was stopping to pick them and had quite a fistful to give to Signora Mazzetti.

Looking closely at her daughter, Bruna thought that she might one day be a pretty girl. Her hair had never been cut, so it was still downy, but Bruna reckoned it would grow to be lush and black like Maria's. Her eyes were big, coloured blue and yellow, the shade peculiar to Artemio's family. They dwarfed her little nose and mouth in a soulful way, and the contrast between them and her dark hair and tanned skin was startling. Bruna gathered the bundle of darning that she planned to do at the Mazzettis' more firmly to her chest and thought that right now Ottavia looked more like one of the little chicks that she cared for so well. All fluffy hair and skinny shins sticking out like bird's legs from under the fullness of her smock dress.

'Quickly now,' Bruna called again when a cool current of air streamed out from the lush dampness inside Artemio's chestnut woods. It was as though someone had opened a larder door onto the summer night's air. It reminded her that this mild evening was one of the season's last.

Already at the Mazzettis' house, Artemio leant up against a tree stump in which red flowers bloomed. He examined his nails while he waited for Bruna and Ottavia, then turned to look at the house, his fingers moving on to twist his moustache. The Mazzetti home was big, appearing even larger because of the barn that was attached to the far wall. On the upper floor were three large bedrooms that for decades had been kept furnished and fresh in preparation for the babies that never came. As the years fell away behind the ageing couple, the few hectares around their house had become harder to farm, until eventually they had to stop. They began instead to rent out their empty bedrooms to passers-by, and over time their home became known as the Ospita (the hospit). Travellers were offered dinner and a bed, as well as access to a small, illegal shop within their kitchen that stocked a few dried goods and cheese. They did relatively well in their enterprise because of the itinerant peddlers and cart drivers who hauled their goods up and down the road that the Brunis and Mazzettis shared, a popular short cut to Stia and Pratovecchio. Whatever they lacked, they received in the form of gifts from Signora Mazzetti's many satisfied customers.

Death in the Mountains

Artemio's friendship with the Mazzettis had had a funny and memorable start which seemed to bond him with the couple all the more tightly. He had initially made their acquaintance at his wedding, then again on the road outside their houses shortly after he'd moved into Poggio. Young and inexperienced, Artemio had told the Mazzettis about his recently purchased ox. Its knee had swollen and he feared it would soon develop a fever. He said he could no sooner afford a veterinarian than any of the medicine the vet would prescribe. Upon hearing of the sick beast, Signora Mazzetti promised to drop over a sure cure. The next night she honoured her pledge and brought over a plate of earthworms soaked in wine. The juicy, long, purple-black worms were to be heated and soaked into a dressing pack for the ox's aching joint. It was late and dark when Artemio finally left the barn for the house, his lantern burning out on the way in. Stumbling about in the kitchen, with only the light of the dying fire to guide him, Artemio felt like having a snack before bed. Thinking that his considerate bride had left him a small meal on the table, Artemio gobbled down Signora Mazzetti's dish without a thought. It was only the next morning when Bruna found the empty plate and called to Artemio to ask if he'd seen the miracle cure that he'd realised what he'd done. The worms had no immediate or long-term effect on his health, though they did put him off his food for quite some time. The Mazzettis and Brunis all became fast friends through the laughs that followed that incident.

And their stories! The Mazzettis always had the best tales at *veglia*. There was not a Tuscan in the world who did not like a good ghost story and there was not a family in Casentino that knew more ghost stories than the Mazzettis. Spectres lived in certain places and the souls of these damned men and animals hovered over particular fields or lurked in the shadows of tracks. Signor Mazzetti had told Artemio all about the calf ghost that mooed in the woods near Il Villaggio's church, beseeching its mother to return with mournful bellows that some had heard with the full moon. There was also the Dark Rider. Signor Mazzetti had actually seen him, moving through the sheep at Omomorto. Artemio had grown up with stories of the Dark Rider, the Florentine man who had falsified money in the 1400s. The man had used his fake money throughout Florence and was on his way to Stia to try his luck there. But a Florentine lynching mob caught up with him and beat him to death by the roadside. The next day a crowd came, dug a hole and threw in his body. From that time forward, anyone who passed by threw a stone onto his makeshift grave. Till this day there is a mountain of rocks beside the road to Stia from Florence and the place took the name of Deadman – Omomorto – to remember the fraudster and his tricks. When Signor Mazzetti saw the Dark Rider pass through the flock, the sheep did not move to make way for him. 'His soul is still there,' the old man maintained. 'He has not gone to the other world.'

Artemio pushed open the Mazzettis' front door and called out a loud *'Buona sera.'* Signor Mazzetti was sitting at the fireplace, soaking up the warmth of the incandescent logs. He looked like a twiggy tree hung with clothes, all folded limbs with a shirt and pants bagging around him. Disturbed from his thoughts, he looked up and smiled.

'Artemio! *Buona sera!* Damp, isn't it?' Signor Mazzetti said, almost apologetically, as though embarrassed at being caught out at feeling old. He rose from his chair with dignity and ushered the Brunis into his home with the wave of a large, big-knuckled hand.

When the door shut, darkness enveloped the room once again. More than five hundred years old, the house had been built when windows were considered a source of cold rather than light. Its walls were pitch, coated with decades of soot from the constantly burning fire. A flinty smell of coal hung in the air, along with the damp that rose in the corners and the gravel dust that fixed itself inside their clothes. As the family moved to the benches in front of the fire, the flames cast flickering shadows behind them.

'I checked my chestnuts and they're good – but not good enough to hire hands to help collect them. What magic did you weave on yours? My wife would certainly like to know,' Signor Mazzetti laughed. 'And you, pretty little one, what flowers you have there! Why don't you take them to the signora in the vegetable garden? I know she would like to see your tiny fingers working beside her.'

'*Si*, Signore.' And Ottavia skipped off. Once she was out of the room, the three adults settled themselves on the benches.

'We will try again tonight?' Signor Mazzetti smiled, revealing in his mouth the lone yellow corn kernel he so wanted to remove.

'I've brought the necessary tools.' Artemio pulled string from his pocket. He'd separated the threads of some work rope to make a strand strong, yet fine, enough to do the job. He wrapped both ends around his index fingers and snapped it sharply so that it twanged.

'To work, then! While the little one's outside, eh?'

Artemio rubbed his whiskers. 'All right. I need a candle.' He had heard of this trick while threshing this summer. He'd been assured it was guaranteed to remove even the most stubborn tooth.

Signor Mazzetti fetched a candle from the table and took it to the fire to light it. He passed it to Bruna, who stood by the fire ready to assist in the operation. All three huddled in front of the flames. Bruna held the candle to one side of the tooth, Artemio fumbled with securing the string around the base of it, and Signor Mazzetti, face trusting and expectant, kept his gummy mouth wide open. It was a fiddly job for Artemio's thick fingers; however, he was good with his hands and not generally given to being clumsy.

'Ready,' Artemio breathed heavily. He held the string taut in his right hand while Bruna passed the candle over to his left. Holding the flame close to the old man's face, Artemio feigned the need to see better. 'Come a little nearer. That's it,' he coaxed, all the while gently pulling the string, as though softly but firmly reeling in a fish.

Leaning forward, the old man stretched his neck out further, closer and closer to the candle. Suddenly Signor Mazzetti jerked his head back. But Artemio was ready and simultaneously tugged sharply on the string.

'AI-YAH! MY NOSE!' Signor Mazzetti yelled. 'You've burnt my nose on that damned candle!'

Artemio looked down at the empty little noose in his hands. 'That's the whole point. You're supposed to pull your head back when the candle burns your nose and pull out your own tooth.'

'Well, did you get it, then?' Signor Mazzetti asked wanly, snaking his tongue up to his gum to feel for his tooth. He looked crestfallen when he discovered it was still there.

'I felt it give. I'm sure it's looser.' Artemio tried to sound encouraging as he slipped the string back in his pocket. 'We'll try again soon, all right?'

'Is it out?' called Signora Mazzetti, flinging open the door, standing expectantly in the doorway. 'I could hear my Marcello from the garden!'

'Not this time, Signora Mazzetti,' responded Bruna as she gave her friend a kiss on each cheek. 'But Artemio says it's been loosened.'

Signora Mazzetti sagged. 'Another night of pain for you, Marcellino.' Then she dropped her voice to a whisper as if her husband were not present in the room. 'He has a lump under the tooth now, you know.' Disappointed, she looked down at the bouquet of wildflowers in her hand. 'I'll make up some strong poppyseed tea and something to draw out the pus in the lump.' As though pulling herself together, she upped her volume, 'Also, I have a gift! From the mother of the Podervecchio boys. The youngest had *il ruzzo*. I sewed him up, though, and she gave me a drop of their wine.'

'*Buono!* Good! That'll help me sleep!' Signor Mazzetti clapped his hands together.

Ottavia wandered in.

'Some water for the little one?'

'Oh, no, no,' answered Ottavia, looking wide-eyed at her mother.

'Ottavia doesn't drink anything before bed,' Bruna said hastily. Though she shared many family concerns with her best friend, she would not tell her that Ottavia had a history of bed-wetting; it was too embarrassing and reflected badly upon her mothering skills. Artemio was more or less oblivious to it, as he cared for the problems of the land and she to those of the family.

'Some tart, then?'

'*Si, grazie*, Signora,' said Ottavia, following Signora Mazzetti over to the *madia* (the low kitchen cupboard used for kneading and storing bread). Signora Mazzetti lifted out of it the classic summer tart. Instead of fresh berries she'd smeared her blackberry jam over the top of the sweet pastry base, then crisscrossed further strips of pastry over the top of the jam. As she busied herself with slicing, the men fell into conversation.

'Giubbotto says he's found a family for Poggio,' Artemio said, pausing to cough and spit. Bruna's head sprang up. He had not shared this information with her.

'Where are they farming now?' asked Signor Mazzetti.

'He wouldn't give that much away. No word on when they'll want to move in, either.'

'They'll get their planting done before they move, just like you. Unless they're not Casentinese, and if they're not, why would they want to be?' The men shared a smile.

Signora Mazzetti started up her own talk. 'What did I want to say? *Allora*, so, the third youngest Podervecchio boy had *il ruzzo* and was giving his mother such a hard time. Always running here, yelling there, thinking only about shirking his work and having a good time. Just like his older brothers, really.'

Bruna tried to listen to Signora Mazzetti while keeping an ear on Artemio and Signor Mazzetti too.

'I put some white thread into a needle and pretended to sew up his eyes, first stitching up, then across, just like Our Lord's crucifix, while saying my prayers. His mother shouldn't have any more problems. He'll calm down now.'

'When are you going up to see your brother?' continued Signor Mazzetti, not listening to his wife.

'I'm not going to. He owes me no favours. There's no reason why he should move out before he has to.'

'You should go up there now and look at all the tools. Things have been known to disappear. Once the *sensale* has sorted out what's yours and what's Sauro's, Sauro should leave.'

'I'll wait. I trust my brother. He would never steal from

me. The *sensale* says he'll come to estimate in late November, when my chestnuts are in.'

'Too late! Too late! It's common sense to go up now, even if you move in January.'

'The *sensale* knows I want to settle my chestnuts before I move.'

'Then organise them but, my friend, go over Campo Alto's tools now, as soon as you can, and ask your brother to leave Campo Alto no later than December, so that you're out of here before the snow falls.'

Artemio looked uncomfortable. It would have been wise to follow his friend's advice and number the tools, and at least check the livestock's condition before he took over Sauro's farm. His conscience also told him to pay a social visit to his brother. He scratched his chin thoughtfully. No, it could all wait until the end of November, when his chestnuts were drying. There should be no distractions from that harvest, it was too important. If the crop was as big as he hoped, there was good money at stake.

'No, I'll leave it.'

Signor Mazzetti shrugged and turned his face away.

'Here, a drop of wine before it rests in the cool room for another night,' declared Signora Mazzetti. With an expert snap of her wrist she flicked out the olive oil that acted as a cork in the neck of the flask. She put tumblers on the table and filled their glasses like a nurse rationing medicine to patients. As hostess she took the first glass of wine, the least palatable because of its traces of olive oil.

'If the little one cannot drink water, here, give her some wine.'

Bruna felt it would be ill-mannered to decline, so passed Ottavia a trickle of wine.

To manage the tart placed on a plate before him, Signor Mazzetti took his knife out of its battered leather case and nicked the tart's crust along the edges to make it easier to gum off bite-size pieces. He sucked loudly with his mouth open, jaws working back and forth, like a small child getting its first taste of a boiled sweet.

The men and women talked concurrently about the topics that interested them. Artemio shared Bruna's idea of bringing his mother and father to Campo Alto to live with them. Signor Mazzetti thought it was a marvellous notion. He knew the house well, as it was visible from the road to Omomorto. He recalled that the kitchen had a veranda. He suggested that Artemio's parents would enjoy eating lunch there on hot days.

Bruna sewed her way through her needlework by candlelight, her diminishing pile revealing sweat-stained singlets and sweaters that looked like empty moulds of her children. She darned Silvio's split pants, patched a jacket and added a panel up the back of an old vest to make it big enough for Mario. Signora Mazzetti knitted a woollen spencer for her husband. A small embroidered image of Jesus with a burning, thorn-encrusted heart lay on the table ready to be stitched onto the spencer's chest, so that His Holy likeness would lie across Signor Mazzetti's heart. Women and girls preferred to wear the Madonna with baby Jesus over their hearts.

The women wondered when Felice, the travelling haberdashery man, would return, as they both needed hooks with eyelets. Signora Mazzetti asked Bruna if she would buy cotton for the boys to make new Sunday shirts. Bruna said no, she would save the money and reinvent a few articles of clothing from a length of hemp she had stored away.

Stretched out on the bench between the women, Ottavia fell asleep, wondering why Signora Mazzetti smelt of boiled grass and why the floor creaked of its own accord, but lulled by the murmuring of the adults.

Veglia concluded in the same fashion as it did in every home across the country – in prayer. Signora Mazzetti led the rosary, as she was the religious head of the household. Eyes closed, the women's nimble fingers clicked off the polished olive pips that served as rosary beads. Signora Mazzetti recited a mystery in Jesus's life, then together they whispered ten Hail Marys in a row, one for every small bead, then one Our Father for every large bead, until they had finished the entire necklace. That made fifty Hail Marys and five Our Fathers. On this night the women went around the rosary only once, though they should have repeated their entreaties many more times. The priest at Il Villaggio encouraged five devout loops each night. That meant reciting two hundred and fifty Hail Marys and twenty-five Our Fathers. On this night, though, the women shared a subtle glance and knew from each other's looks that they were both too weary to continue. The men stayed silent throughout, looking down at their hands with varying degrees of piety as the rosary drew to a close.

Then, with warm goodnights and a kiss to the top of Ottavia's head, Bruna and Artemio walked out into the night.

Early the next morning, when Bruna popped outside to give baby Pasquale a crust of bread, Maria appeared battle-wounded. Spurts of blood-red liquid looked like lacerations across her cheeks and gashes up her arms. She was sitting on a chair just outside the front door with a pyramid of mature tomatoes on her lap. A further eight crates of tomatoes leant in a crooked column by her side. With a knife that she wished was serrated, she methodically worked her way through each tomato, slicing them one at a time before tossing them in pieces into a *paiolo,* a big copper cooking pot.

Under Bruna's supervision, Maria was making the Brunis' tomato *conserva,* a preparation for winter undertaken at the close of every summer. Poggio was only a small farm, so the first of Maria's two, maybe three, pots of concentrated tomato preserve would be over the fire to boil by ten that morning and the job finished by the afternoon.

The bigger farms, however, down in the valley of Florence or in the hills across the province of Tuscany, with their large extended families, would make considerably more *conserva.* Their method, along with the number of women needed to do the job, was quite different from that of the Casentinese. They first boiled their tomatoes with salicylic acid (a food preservative found to be harmful and banned in the United States around this time), filtered out the seeds and skins, then poured the tomatoes onto sheets that had been stretched tightly across the seats of several wooden chairs, their straw bases removed. Once the excess moisture had dripped through the material into buckets placed below the chairs, the tomatoes dried into a dense, jellylike strips that could be lifted off and rolled up like scrolls. When needed, the *conserva* was sliced and melted in warm water before it was eaten with dishes such as *frittata trippata,* a farmer's recipe of fried chopped onion, celery, carrots, dried summer herbs and diluted tomato preserve, tossed through a thinly sliced omelette. The end result was a meal that resembled pasta, only *frittata trippata* was served on thick slices of bread.

Bruna Bruni's ruby mixture, which Maria copied, was less time-consuming. The tomatoes were boiled, the acid added and the water that formed at the top of the pot periodically

Death in the Mountains

scooped out till the *conserva* was reduced to a thick pulp. It was then sieved through wire netting and poured into clay containers shaped like miniature pot-belly stoves and sealed with olive oil. A few kilos were kept aside till the next bread-making day, when it was poured into a dish and baked inside the oven. That *conserva* became a thick jelly, so concentrated that Bruna lifted it out with a knife and sliced it into cubes, adding it perhaps to a skillet of onions, sage and rabbit. Sometimes she mixed it into a boiling bean and garlic stew or stirred it through smoked cod and potatoes.

As Maria chopped, she asked baby Pasquale the odd question or two. He sat on a shawl on the grass across from her, propped up against an empty crate, almost delirious with joy at having his legs free of their bindings. 'Are you hot with that jacket across your legs?' 'You're almost a big boy now, aren't you?' 'You'll not choke on that crust, eh?'

Maria liked that he could not answer, as she was not eager to engage in conversation. She preferred silence and, at sixteen years old, knew herself well enough to know that she was more at ease on her own than in company. People, with their senseless prattle, stole her calm. Maria preferred the countryside and felt that the land's honesty and quiet were a part of her. Conversing with others, their questions, chatter, all of it jarred the stillness inside her.

That said, Maria was neither aloof nor unfriendly. On the contrary. She was warm and giving, the kind of girl who would say yes to anything you asked, for fear that a no might hurt or upset you. Her soft blue eyes had no challenge in their gaze, more than likely because of her years of solitude in the woods with the animals. After such isolation she had no inclination to share company, and even if she had, her extraordinary beauty made it difficult for others to talk to her.

It was not part of the Tuscan culture to grant women nicknames as readily as men, unless, of course, like Maria, they possessed something that set them apart. L'Angelo, the farmers called her – the Angel ('angel' in Italian always ends with the male vowel). This was because she had the rare kind of exquisiteness that people stood back and enjoyed. They liked to say that their eyes wandered aimlessly until they lit upon the Angel's face; then they could rest there, as though on a perfect flower.

Sadly, though, loveliness, like any characteristic that sets people apart, draws much unwanted attention, and Maria often found herself the object of that ugly emotion jealousy. Coveting another girl's beauty was a big problem among the *signorine* in country Tuscany, and so many girls looked at her through envious eyes. This was no small matter, because some might cast the evil eye or make voodoo dolls as revenge against her.

Maria's mother and Signora Mazzetti were well aware of the threat. They knew what a jealous maiden could do, so they were happy to keep Maria at home as much as possible, especially after Artemio had taken his eldest daughter to the markets at Stia a couple of times. On both occasions the staring had been so unpleasant that he resolved to do something completely out of character – consult Bruna about it. He told her how Maria's loveliness had made the men and women lock eyes on her as if she were a freak. It was not that the stares were lewd. The older men did not leer at her in a sexual way, maybe because part of her attractiveness was her chaste humility, a pure Madonna-like innocence that they revered. The young boys just gawked, awkwardly tripping over their feet and bumping into cartwheels as she passed. The signoras, or matrons, on the other hand, looked surprised. They narrowed their eyes at her while their own young daughters looked over their shoulders with whispering mouths barely concealed by jittery hands.

The whole affair had made Artemio's emotions swing like a clacking metronome. As he'd looked around and noticed the lingering eyes, his emotions had changed from pride to protectiveness, till he was engulfed by a wary kind of anxiety that made him angry. Bruna told him simply that there was nothing at the markets that gave nearly so much pleasure as Maria's face and that people would always be drawn to pleasure. But to avoid the curses of the dark arts, she decided that Maria should be allowed out only to help harvest their neighbours' crops, and only when accompanied by Mario. Thus, Maria found herself in exile because of her beauty.

On the clear, crisp morning of *conserva* day, the day after *veglia* at the Mazzettis', Bruna had gone outside to oversee Maria's progress with the tomatoes and give a crust to baby Pasquale. She left them there and returned inside, the baby sucking on his bread with gurgles of glee. The rest of the family had left for the fields, woods and mountainside after breakfast, Silvio to retie the long, unruly beans back onto their poles, Anna to run the pigs and Fiamma the sheep, while Artemio and Mario ploughed the wheatfield after having burnt off the roots. Bruna had stayed behind, wanting to set Maria and the baby up with the *conserva* before cleaning the house and joining the men.

Once back inside the house Bruna enjoyed its drowsy stillness. The ash she collected from the fireplace floated like dust motes in the ribbons of light from the kitchen window. She put the ash, as white and as fine as talcum powder, into a rag and tied it with string. Filling an empty pail with hot water she dropped the pouch of ash into the water and let it rest there. Shortly she returned to it, dipping the pouch in and out, in and out, till the steaming water was opaque and thick with the strained ash. The water and ash had combined now to become soap – *il ranno*. Bruna dipped another rag into the *ranno* and began to scrub at the gritty oil stains around the stone sink till they lifted. Grime had accumulated at the back of the sink where a hole sloped through the wall to flow the dirty sink water out into the backyard. She wrapped her finger in the rag, dipped it again into the slippery water and jiggled her finger around the hole till the scum slid away. Moving through the kitchen, she added more *ranno* to the tabletop to rid it of the smell of the children's raw onion and tomato breakfast.

She was thinking how she had to keep enough of the velvety potion aside for baby Pasquale's nappy strips when she stopped to listen to Maria calling her. There was concern in her voice.

'Mamma! Mamma! Signora Mazzetti is coming with Ottavia!'

Bruna felt a jolt of alarm as she made her way to the door, rag still in hand. She could see Signora Mazzetti marching up the track with Ottavia dragging her feet behind. Bruna saw from Ottavia's obvious despondency and her friend's briskness what had happened. Ottavia had been thrown out of the Mazzetti home for wetting her bed. Bruna was mortified. She felt the shame rise in her chest and become heat in her face. As if to try to contain it she crossed her arms, rag and all, across her chest.

Nearing the house, Signora Mazzetti called out. 'My dear Bruna. You should have told me the child had a problem.'

Bruna clutched at her heart as the guilt washed over her.

How could Ottavia have done this to her dearest friend? Signora Mazzetti was too old to lift and dry her mattress. It took great effort for her to wash her sheets. Her enormous copper pot had to be filled with litres of water and a fire lit underneath it. The Mazzetti bedroom would smell of her daughter's urine for months. Bruna began to wail, inconsolable.

'Forgive me! Oh, Holy Mary, Mother of God, comfort me now. I should never have sent this wretch to you!' Bruna cried. 'I am such a fool! Pride. That is my sin. I was too proud to tell you of my daughter's troubles.'

Ottavia, frightened by her mother's reaction, began to sob and hid behind Signora Mazzetti.

'May the Lord punish me for my selfishness. I should have told you,' Bruna cried, pulling at her hair. 'Come out, you wicked girl,' she shrieked, turning her attention to Ottavia, trying to reach around Signora Mazzetti to catch her.

Ottavia dodged her mother's lunges by darting about the elderly woman, who, it must be said, was having difficulty seeing what was going on – her back was so bent she had trouble looking up, never mind keeping track of a frightened child dashing this way and that.

'The indignity! How could you do this to our dear Mazzettis and to us? How could you shame your family like this?' Bruna grabbed Ottavia by the collar and yanked her away from the protection of the signora's full skirt. She could see the child's dress was soiled, stained dark with urine. A lingering smell of stale piss hovered around her.

'My dear ...' Signora Mazzetti tried to soothe.

Bruna held Ottavia tightly around the shoulders, lifted her grief-stricken face towards the sky and began moaning a prayer.

'Listen ... Bruna ... BRUNA!' yelled Signora Mazzetti finally.

Bruna looked at her, as if coming to her senses. Then she glanced around. Maria was watching her mother, in disbelief, while baby Pasquale had begun to hiccup. Bruna could see Silvio in the vegetable patch, his arms suspended, as though frozen in midair while disentangling the beans, staring at her. Then she saw that Artemio and Mario were running towards them from the fields.

'Come. Let Ottavia go. Follow me,' ordered Signora Mazzetti before turning towards the panicked men. 'Go back to the fields!' she called with a commanding gesture, as though she were pushing them backwards. The men slowed their run before stopping to watch from a distance. 'Go on. Return to your work! Everything is fine here. Do not worry.'

Reluctantly, Artemio and Mario turned around and walked back to their ploughing. They were clearly surprised. Ordinarily, Bruna was difficult to fluster. She was known for being a hard-headed, steady woman. From her weeping, they thought that something terrible had happened. They did not know that for Bruna, Ottavia's overnight incontinence was a betrayal. The men did not understand that the whole affair made her out to be a terrible mother and an even worse friend.

'Maria, Ottavia. Stay outside.'

Gently, as though leading an indisposed person back to their sickbed, Signora Mazzetti took Bruna's arm and led her into the house.

Bruna sniffed, wringing her hands. 'Oh, Blessed Lord! Forgive us, Signora Mazzetti. I did not think ... I had hoped ...' The old lady shushed her with two upheld palms. 'I'll hear no more about it,' interrupted Signora Mazzetti. 'How long has this been going on?'

'Always, but not every day.'

'The child's condition is obvious. She wets herself while asleep because her kidneys are soiled. They must be purified. For goodness sake, you should have told me. Bruna, we must cure her!'

'Dirty kidneys?' asked Bruna, looking incredulous.

'Yes. You must catch a mouse … tonight! Skin it. Roast it. The little one must eat it tomorrow. Only a mouse can cure fouled kidneys.' Bruna opened her mouth to say something, but again Signora Mazzetti silenced her. 'Tonight. Catch a mouse. And you'll have no more pissings.'

After sunset Bruna went to the barn to set the trap, an old wooden cage with wooden slats. The cantankerous contraption slammed shut its trapdoor of iron struts when the cheese and the string around it were tampered with. As Bruna fiddled, the barn cat looked at her with slitty-eyed suspicion.

As there was no shortage of field vermin at Poggio, the next morning there were two mice in her trap. Bruna decided to make extra sure the cure worked, and so, carefully she lifted the pelt off both mice. She gutted them, cut off their heads and feet and stuffed them with garlic and rosemary. She laid the mice side by side in a covered terracotta baking dish, poured olive oil over them and pushed them deep into the burning coals of the fire.

Called to the table before everyone else, Ottavia came timidly.

'I have a special meal just for you, little one,' said Bruna softly, stroking her daughter's hair. 'Two little birdies to make you big and strong.'

Ottavia felt the meal was a lovely treat and her mother's way of saying sorry. Bruna stayed by her daughter's side throughout, encouraging her to nibble all the meat off the bones. Ottavia happily ate her 'little birdies' all up.

Later, the end to the torment of Ottavia's bed-wetting would be viewed with wonder – yet another amazing cure provided by the inimitable Signora Mazzetti. As promised by Bruna's dear old friend, Ottavia never wet her bed again.

7

September

Squeak-eek, eek-squeak went the furry sage leaves as they rubbed against the girl's teeth. Fiamma squinched up her nose at the spicy taste but scrubbed for all she was worth because her mother had all four girls under surveillance as they brushed their teeth in the courtyard. They stood in a row, bending forward, clenching thick bunches of sage to their mouths in concentration. '*Eh, eh, shpuut,*' they spat, and then smacked their lips with satisfaction at the new smoothness of their teeth. Many Casentinese used coal for their oral hygiene. They crushed it up on kitchen tables with their irons and rubbed it into their teeth with their fingers. But Bruna Bruni did not care for coal; she said it set her teeth on edge. So it was sage the family used for their Sunday ablutions before church.

On this early autumn morning, Bruna's face was sterner than usual. The weather had changed fast over the last few days and there was still much to be done, not the least of which was this last bathing session. Getting wet when bedroom breath was as thick as smoke, and icicles like knives hung from the ceiling, led to the fevers, pneumonia and death. Today's full body wash would do the children for the next eight or nine months.

Bruna's apprehension over her children getting wet was more real now than a week ago. The patches of bare ground around the farm had been dry and hard then. Now they were moist all day long, unwilling to let go of the night's dew. At dawn the damp cold nipped greedily at the Brunis' noses, and sunset came earlier, bringing shadows with tingling chills inside them. This sudden onset of autumn had taken Bruna by surprise and made her feel as though all undertakings now needed to be rushed. The stream water would be like ice for her daughters (and they would be followed by her sons), but she could not remedy that, only speed them along as much as possible.

'Go, go,' she commanded while herding them towards an assembled pile of cleansing materials. Maria, Anna and Fiamma each grabbed something as they passed it. Two rags, a bottle of vinegar, a pail of water boiled with nettles, a pail of *ranno* (cleaning solution), an empty pail that held four yellowing cotton towels similar to shrunken sheets with tassels, and four pairs of fresh underwear. Bruna had not bothered to include soap as she knew they would not use it. Made from the Christmas pig's fat and caustic soda, it stung their eyes and irritated their skin.

'*Presto, presto*. Quickly, hurry up, Ottavia, or they'll leave you behind,' she warned. Spitting out the last of her sage, Ottavia picked up her skirts and ran to the top of the path that led to the sword slash down to the stream. Anna held out her hand for her and together they scrabbled down, gathering speed as they went, buckets and jugs sloshing their contents onto their legs.

'Shhh, quiet, everyone. Let's see if we can catch them,' whispered Fiamma. They slowed their pace, pausing and creeping, quietly panting from the scramble down. Most mornings the deer came to this part of the creek and if the girls were quiet they could catch them, front legs splayed, having a drink. Sometimes there were whole families of wild boar: black, hairy males with playful babies that rolled in the mud while their mothers stood by grunting. Cautiously they navigated the brook's banks, coming gradually to the spot where it widened into a slow-moving pool. Midges hovered on its rippling surface. Grey tadpoles whizzed in its crystal depths. But no wild animals this morning.

'We're too late. Oh, a pity,' said Anna, looking around her, still hopeful that a baby deer was hiding nearby. They stayed quiet for a few more minutes, listening for the telltale rustling of leaves. Anna gave an involuntary shiver and put down her bucket. Branches crowded the sky above them, forbidding any direct sunlight onto the little waterhole. Its banks were moist; the frigid water clung to the very air around them.

'*Vai, muoviamoci.* Come on, let's get moving.' The feeling that they had better make haste came over Anna too. All four girls began to take off their headscarves and step out of their shoes.

'*Prima io! Prima io!* Me first! Me first!' sang Ottavia.

'*Si, si, oh ... per carità! Aspetta!* Yes, yes ... oh, for charity's sake! Wait!' responded Fiamma with a dramatic roll of her eyes. 'You're always first.' Then Fiamma slipped on some clammy autumn leaves that hugged the moss-covered stones at the water's edge. '*Accidenti alla miseria, sei una peste!* The pox on poverty, you are a nuisance!'

'Come here,' called Anna softly. Gently she took out the little girl's plaits. She unbuttoned Ottavia's smock and lifted that, along with her undershirt, over her head.

As far as the personalities of the Bruni children were concerned, it was commonly thought that they could be split into two different groups – Mario, Fiamma (the name means flame) and Ottavia because they shared a fire in their bellies; and Maria, Anna and Silvio because they had a demure countenance.

Anna, their mother's favourite, was thirteen years old and had already passed eight years on the hillsides; like Maria, the isolation had made her as quiet as the lambs she tended. Throughout the summer now passed, Anna had blossomed into a young lady. She had stretched, hardened and budded. With the changes in her body came the understanding that she would never be as lovely as Maria, no matter how much they were paired and compared. This realisation did not make her envious, for, just like a young tree, she bent to the blows of nature and then unfurled herself, changed only in that she was stronger, grittier and better prepared to face any further harsh surprises.

Maria, Anna and Silvio were also similar in feeling a deep love of the land. They breathed the air and thought of the weather; they watched each broom bush, chestnut and cherry tree as if they were childhood confidants, silently acknowledging them as they passed. They understood nature – that if the older trees were cut, they took longer to heal, if indeed they ever did, just like older people; that the younger trees could withstand an accidental lop, scar and get better. They were uncomplicated children, inherently content with their lives.

These characteristics were not shared by Fiamma, who, her father said, walked about the farm with her eyes open but her senses closed. Even at eleven years old it was clear that

Fiamma was a firebrand. She had no qualms about voicing her opinions, while Maria and Anna felt guilty about even *having* opinions. She felt entitled to ask and to have; the other two felt comfortable only when doing without. When folding sheets, she decided which corner had to be met with the left or right. She thought it was her unquestioned right to sprinkle the pinenuts on the sweet chestnut slice, her right to name the lambs. She had her way among her sisters because, when all was said and done, Fiamma was a very funny little girl. She found humour in even the most odious tasks and made them fun for the others. She had a keen sense of the Tuscan tease, so when sleeping out in the wealthy Casentinese homes in domestic service she had made friends among the other farm girls. Fiamma could be unreasonable and demanding one minute and a trickster with a knack for mimicry the next.

Silvio was a sweet nine-year-old boy whom everybody liked. He spoke little and wore a wide smile to hide his shyness. If he had trouble finding the right words when out with the farmers, he also had an endearing mop of black hair that women couldn't resist ruffling. More than anything, Silvio was known for his penchant for taking off his shoes. One day the key to the barn door fell off into his clogs. Artemio was cross with him when the key appeared lost and made Silvio search for it through the fields and the hay. The soles of his feet were so tough that only when going to bed that night did Silvio find the key inside his shoe. Long, thick and made of iron, it had been there all day and he had not even felt it.

Kept separate from the children because of his age and differing jobs was Mario. Although he spent very little time with the girls now, doing the work that demanded strength, there had been a time when he had seen them often. That was a dreadful period for the girls. It was when they were tiny and gullible, naive enough to believe whatever he said, too raw to know that he was born with a malicious sense of humour. Mario played tricks on them that only he thought were funny.

When he'd filled up a sack with stones and told Maria to take it back to their mother, he'd laughed all evening. Thinking the bag was full of chestnuts, Maria had developed blisters from lugging the rocks from the woods to the house, only to be scoffed at for her silliness by her mother. Mario chafed poison ivy into the girls' sheets so that their skin rashed burgundy with irritation. He chipped Silvio's hoe handle so that tiny wooden shards came away and splintered his palm while he worked. On all these occasions Mario laughed hard, while Maria, Anna, Fiamma and Silvio squirmed in discomfort and, eventually, fear. Encouraged by his sisters because he was a boy, so therefore more likely to be taken seriously, Silvio told their father of Mario's pranks. Artemio thought his elder son's tricks would sharpen the children and ignored Silvio's complaints. The next day, when grazing the sheep in the melting snow by the road, kilometres from home, Silvio's clothes fell apart. Out of revenge, Mario had unpicked the stitches in his jacket and pants, knowing that his brother would, quite literally, freeze.

By the time Ottavia and baby Pasquale were born, Mario had moved on to other pursuits, such as *veglia* at certain farms near Poggio. He did his work, ate, and left the house. The girls and Silvio heaved a sigh of relief when his jacket disappeared from the coat rack. When he was gone, their home became safer, but he'd left his legacy. Their big brother's cruelty had made the other Bruni children fit together like a forged chain; they were linked by fear of him, but when they were together they felt strong.

Stripped down now to her drawstring underpants, little Ottavia jiggled up and down for warmth. Goosebumps rose on her skin till she looked like a freshly plucked chicken. Maria and Anna dipped rags into the *ranno* and began to splash her body down with it. They scrubbed at her neck, knees and elbows while Ottavia yelped with the cold. When they tipped a bucket of water over her head to rinse her off, she screamed at the top of her lungs before laughing wildly through chattering teeth. Before long they had her hair washed with the nettle water and rinsed with vinegar, and had sat her on a rock, wrapped in a towel. Anna handed her a smooth river-worn stone. Ottavia knew the routine – she was to scrub her toes and fingers with it till they were pasty white. She began by flicking off the flecks of moss that stuck to her ankles like an invasion of green ants.

'Did Babbo tell you when we are moving?' Anna asked Maria as they ran the rags over their bodies as quickly as possible.

'He'll see Uncle Sauro soon,' responded Maria uneasily. The thought of moving made her fearful, as did most things that meant change. She would miss Poggio terribly.

'I want to know when we are going. Why can't he tell us when we'll move? I heard mamma tell Signora Mazzetti that Campo Alto will make us lots of money,' said Fiamma, swinging from a whine to excitement in one breath.

'There'll be no money for us. Babbo is saving every lira for his own land. That's what mamma says.' Their underpants were dark with water now. They felt their nakedness keenly and did not like to bath completely nude. With shaky fingers they rinsed each other's hair and scrutinised each other's bodies. They'd never seen themselves bare, so each regarded her sister's body as a mirror reflection of her own.

'Oh, Anna! Look at your *poppe*! They're so big now!' called Fiamma with glee. Ashamed, Anna covered her pear-shaped breasts with clumps of long wet hair.

'You'll be old soon,' Fiamma went on, 'and, like Signora Mazzetti, you will not be able to wear underpants because you'll only be able to do pee pee standing up. Signora Mazzetti told Ottavia that if she crouched down, she'd never be able to get back up again. She'd be stuck on the ground like a beetle on its back.'

The girls giggled and shivered and sniffled and laughed until they were sitting on the rise behind the stream's banks, drying off in the sun, all but swallowed by the reedy grass. They ran combs Artemio had carved through their hair. It was a rare moment of freedom and they were in no rush to get back home.

'Why do they call Mario "Trincia"?'

Fiamma, who was still talking about growing old, stopped mid-sentence. Ottavia's question had caught them all by surprise. Anna looked sideways at Maria, craning her neck, so that little Ottavia would not see her trying to catch her sister's eye for a clue as to how to respond.

A shadow seemed to fall over Maria. She worried her fingers inside the tucks of her dress and felt the warmth of the friction from her thumb as it massaged where her index finger had once been. The stump was smooth and shiny. Her mother had stretched the skin across the bloody exposed joint when she had run home from the wheatfields, Fiamma and Anna close behind, gagging with shock. Her sisters had seen her question Mario over his swigs from a hidden wine flask. They'd seen his hand come up as if to hit her, his face puce with rage. They'd watched as she'd thought to protect herself from his blow, only to see his other hand come up and his scythe slice through the air.

'The sickle ...' she had sobbed as her mother dressed her wound, hushed her tight to her breast and rocked her back and forth. It had not been her intention to be dishonest with her mother then; the lie came to her lips when Mario's silhouette loomed in the doorway. She'd recognised the threat in the hunch of his shoulders. It was as if his head were set too tightly into them, like a cork screwed into the neck of a too tight bottle that threatened to explode. She thought then that he was capable of killing her, should she tell their parents how she had lost her finger.

As to why the local farmers called Mario 'Trincia' – *trinciare* meant to mince, cut or shred – she had no idea. Only she, Anna and Fiamma knew what had happened that day. At some point she would tell Ottavia the truth. She would warn her, as knowing what Mario could do when provoked would protect her. But not yet. As far as the farmers went, she imagined that with their usual uncanny irony, they had innocently stumbled onto Mario's nickname.

'Well,' said Maria, pulling her thoughts back to her little sister, 'I'm not sure, but you know how Mario is the swiftest with the sickle at harvest? How his sheaves pile higher than anyone else's by lunchtime?'

Ottavia nodded thoughtfully.

'No one can match him. So I think that's why they call him Trincia.'

Ottavia absorbed this answer and accepted it.

Just then Silvio's voice came echoing down the valley – it was time for the boys to wash in the stream. Their moment of freedom over, the girls quickly packed up their buckets and went home the long way, up through the sloping field that led through the family's front paddock.

On Sunday mornings the local parishes in Tuscany chimed their bells at five o'clock to wake the housewives for the six o'clock mass that was said especially for them. They worshipped before their families so that they would have time to cook lunch and ready their children for church. On some Sundays and all feast days, the women served meat, which took more time to prepare than weekday meals, as the rabbits or chickens had to be slaughtered and skinned. As well as the main meat dish, the pasta had to be made, stretched across the kitchen table and sliced into crooked lines called *maccheroni*. They were left out in the sun on tea towels to dry in time for one o'clock.

The women also had to tend to their rabbits, the animal that each of them held closest to their hearts. Of all the creatures on their farm, only the rabbits belonged solely to Bruna. The oxen belonged to Artemio; the sheep, pigs, ducks and chickens all belonged to the farm's owner. If a rabbit died, the woman of the household had no one to answer to, whereas if the smallest gosling died, even while hatching, its value was subtracted from the farmer's annual payment to the farm's owner.

When Bruna had returned from mass that morning she'd lit the fire, killed a rabbit, prepared her children's breakfast and bathing materials, then skinned and chopped the rabbit. While the children ate, she'd kneaded the pasta, leaving it in a ball under a cloth when she shepherded the girls down to the stream. Once they'd gone and the boys had been mustered to collect firewood, Bruna rolled the dough out across the kitchen table. Baby Pasquale lay on the floor on his back, content to watch his mother move around the kitchen.

With a small shovel, Bruna pulled the burning coals to the front of the hearth and put her iron tripod on top of them. She placed her big terracotta pot on the tripod, pouring into it olive oil and finely chopped onion, celery and carrot. After letting the three vegetables sizzle slowly for a while, she added half a cup of water, then the rabbit pieces. The tender kidneys she would chop for baby Pasquale to suck on. While the rabbit cooked she cut the pasta, carried it outside to dry and collected a fistful of parsley. Finally she pulled the rabbit pieces out, removed all the bones and chopped the meat up finely with the *mezzaluna*, the two-handled knife shaped like a half-moon. She put the meat back into the pot to let the sauce simmer, before putting baby Pasquale to her breast for a feed.

When the church bells rang nine times and baby Pasquale seemed to want to doze, Bruna thought to go up beyond the chestnut woods to the little plateau where the sheep were grazed during the week. If she went up now, she could find the last of the season's clover and some dry grass for her rabbits. With the land so freshly damp she would more than likely find some *porcini* mushrooms too. The fire would burn itself out by the time the meat was ready.

The baby had fallen asleep, so, taking him and an extra jacket in one arm, her kitchen knife and a hessian sack in the other, Bruna went to the chicken coop to collect Pasquale's rabbit cage. She could hear Ottavia's squeals from the stream as she put the jacket and the baby inside the cage and carried him to a grassy spot in the orchard. He would be happier out in the open, she thought, snoozing and gazing at the rustling leaves as they danced in the breeze and reflected the sunshine, safe in his wooden and wire-netted box. Too heavy to carry to the fields or plateau now, she often left him in the rabbit cage. In winter she tended to lie him down on the floor, in front of the grate. In either place she knew that nothing could get to him, and heaven knew he could bring no harm upon himself. Swaddled as tightly as Jesus in the manger, baby Pasquale was completely immobile from his armpits down to his ankles, thanks to his strips of cotton.

Satisfied that he was comfortable and the rabbit cage securely fastened, Bruna walked up the track from the house to the road. In the sky above her, hundreds of swallows screeched and wheeled. They broke formation, dived and dipped, then flapped their wings into a unified V again. She'd been told the swallows went to countries called Tunisia and Algeria for the winter. She did not know if that was true, but did know that there was no greater confirmation that the real cold would be with them soon. She would not see the swallows again till March or April next year. They would return to their summer nests in the ceiling of her barn and she would know then that the mornings would no longer be crystallised by frost. Breathing a goodbye to the birds, she crossed the road and passed through the chestnut woods and climbed the rocky track onto the plateau. From there she looked out upon her world, Il Villaggio's tiny church with its pointy steeple and smattering of houses built on common walls for warmth, in the other direction Poggio and the Ospita.

Odd. There was Il Rosso at the Mazzettis' threshold. She could see Signor Mazzetti standing with one hand on the door, the other on the door frame, as if barring Il Rosso's way. The Mazzettis did not like Il Rosso any more than the Brunis did. Signor Mazzetti seemed unsure of himself. She could tell he was reticent by the way he scratched his chest, then behind his head. What could Il Rosso possibly want with her friends? Bruna's hand unconsciously went down to pat the long skirt under her apron. The seam down the outside of her thigh hid a deep pocket. In it she kept all the family's money. Artemio was good like that, handing the profits over to her silently, both of them hoping that one day they would find they had enough lira for their own land. She kept her hand on the money and watched as Il Rosso explained something to Signor Mazzetti. Soon enough the redhead turned away and Bruna harrumphed as she continued on her way to the plateau.

More than an hour later, her sack full of grass but not as much clover as she'd hoped, Bruna did a last search for *porcini* around some jutting stones. Nothing. It was too early. She would come back soon, though; she could tell the ground was ready to give them up. Taking another ten minutes to gather her knife and sack, Bruna headed back to the house.

'Oh, no!' she muttered. As she drew closer to the orchard, baby Pasquale's crying became louder and louder.

'My poor little boy,' she soothed upon seeing his swollen face. From his puffy eyes and tear-soaked collar, she knew that he'd been crying since she'd left. Exhausted from his exertions, he let out a convulsing whimper upon sight of his mother.

'Come here, we'll make you some bread soup, eh?' She unlatched the cage and eased him out, leaving the clover on the ground. 'We have to feed our rabbits too, though, no?' She gave him a gentle squeeze as he gazed up at her through sad, watery eyes. She supposed, at eighteen months old, he was ready to walk. The very thought of it made her cringe.

'I guess that's enough of the salami wrap then,' she whispered in his ear. She knew it was time to set him free; only, if she took him out of his bindings permanently, her liberty, instead of his, would be severely curtailed. The problem was that over the summer she had on several occasions left him with Maria, letting him kick his legs a little too often in the sun, while Maria carried on with her work. He had become accustomed to the freedom and knew now that he wanted his legs unrestrained all the time.

Bruna had kept all her children in salami wrap (the description came from the saying *'sembra un salamino'* – 'he looks like a little salami'), till they were around eighteen months old. She did this for two important reasons. Firstly, she was a firm believer in leg and hip straightening. When infants arrived, all pink and malleable, she believed their legs and floppy hips needed to be set right. Swaddling was an age-old custom and Bruna was a stickler for tradition. Secondly, binding a baby and placing him in an empty rabbit cage were the only childcare options she had.

Taking him back to the kitchen, Bruna kept baby Pasquale up on her shoulder while she made him his *pappa* (baby food) – a slice of bread mashed in water with olive oil, salt and tiny pieces of cheese. Next year Artemio's parents would be making the *pappa*, she thought, heating the mixture on top of the dying flames. When they moved in, they would take on much of baby Pasquale's care. She smiled as she imagined that they would probably make up some extra baby food for themselves, eating without teeth being so difficult. Bruna looked forward to their company enormously. She had never had the help of an extended family. The farmers said, 'The elderly watch the children until the children are old enough to watch the elderly.' The old were the best babysitters. No longer able to go into the fields for manual work, they took on the youngest children joyfully, because they wanted to be, needed to be, useful. They happily tottered around after the toddlers, knowing that their presence was essential for the family to endure. They taught the children how to cut the *saggina* tree, binding the branches that grew like firecrackers out of its trunk into a broom's head, and how to thread mushrooms, plait garlic and pick out tomato seeds. Her own grandparents had taught her how to weave, so that now she could fix or make the baskets and trays that filled the chestnut drying house. The aged kept the fires burning and the water boiling while the strong ploughed, planted and reaped. The presence of Artemio's parents around Campo Alto would take the strain off Bruna. She no longer felt uncomfortable about Artemio taking over his brother's farm. She was convinced that along with taking in her parents-in-law, it was the right thing to do. Leaving Signora Mazzetti behind would be the most difficult part of their relocation. But she would send Mario down with the oxen to bring her back up to stay with them at Campo Alto as often as possible.

Spoon-feeding the baby, she thought that she could ask Mario to make Pasquale a walker. He had his father's skills with the carving knife and it was easy enough. Just cut the straw out of the seat of a chair and saw down the legs. That way she could carry the walker and the baby out to work with her.

When the girls tumbled in dry from the stream with no snuffles or runny noses, Bruna crossed herself, clasped her hands and thanked the Madonna. She then prepared their clothes and, when the boys came back, repeated her thanks before laying their clothes out too. Confident that they all looked their best, the girls without their aprons, the boys with clothes that had no patches, the Bruni family, without Bruna, walked up to church together.

As always, they passed Il Rosso's house on the way to mass. His family was coming out of their front door in answer to the bells that gave fifteen minutes' notice that the service was about to begin. No one said *Buon giorno*. Il Rosso and his wife had only one child, a seventeen-year-old boy with hair even brassier than his father's. As the Brunis passed, the boy stared at Maria.

8

From side on, Mario Bruni had quite a handsome profile. His eyes were deep set and, in an arresting Romanesque way, his nose straight and strong. It was only when he turned to look at you directly that you realised his face was too narrow and his eyes too deep, as though sunken because they'd fallen off the cliff that was his brow. The effect, when one was anticipating a good-looking young man, was unsettling. Sometimes girls tried to get a better look at him and, aware of this, he accommodated them and could not understand why they rapidly blinked before turning away.

He held himself ramrod straight. He did not loll about like the other farm boys. On the cusp of manhood, they seemed to spend their time waiting for something, as though life started tomorrow, not now. The boys of his age sat on the walls that lined the church's tiny piazza, like crows waiting for the twitch of a worm's head. Mario fancied himself a modern man and when he *andava in giro* (went around) socialising he made sure he appeared busy and in demand, just like a modern man should. That's why he reckoned he sometimes caught a signorina's eye. As to why they turned away, he guessed they thought he was beneath them because as the son of a *mezzadro* he would always be a *mezzadro*.

Mario changed his grip on the rope that went from his hands to the yoke, to the rings in the noses of Artemio's two oxen. He was driving them down to Podervecchio with Maria, Anna, Fiamma and Silvio to husk corn. The day's work would earn each of them a container of corn and enough leaves to change the stuffing inside the family's three mattresses. The corn would be ground into the winter's polenta provisions. Holding the reins with one hand, Mario leant down to pick up the jacket that lay between his feet. Shrouded inside was a wine flask. He gripped the jacket's collar around the bottle, lifted it to his mouth, popped the cork with his teeth and took several long swigs. He planned to finish this flask today and have his friends at Podervecchio refill it for the trip home. It would then be buried in the corner of the barn along with his fifteen lira and the fob-watch chain he'd found laced in between the cobblestones outside the Stia town hall.

He wiped his mouth with his sleeve and glanced behind him at his brother and sisters. They would say nothing. He doubted that they'd even noticed. He'd become much more adept at concealing his drinking these days. They were looking at the countryside that plunged away beside them. The three girls held hands and stared steadfastly at the view. Silvio had taken his shoes off and was daydreaming. The road was narrow, just wide enough for two oxen and the *treggia* (a Tuscan cart with no wheels) that they dragged behind them.

Like a giant sled it grated and ground against the road's stones. The children and the gifts they held took up all the space on its base of thick wicker. Mario turned towards the road ahead and resumed his thoughts, warmed by the wine.

As always, it was Florence that filled his head. Her piazzas had Goliath-like statues that turned into fountains with naked water nymphs at their feet. She had two, or was it three, superb bridges that stretched across the Arno River. From America, modern technology was spreading its fingers across her black, perfectly chiselled streets, with automobiles and electric trams. He'd never seen an automobile, had never even been to Florence. Actually, Mario had not been further than Pratovecchio, the town after Stia, but he'd seen the postcards of Florence tacked up on the wall of his father's favourite bar in Stia. The reddish-brown images of Piazza della Signoria, the Duomo and Via Calzaiuoli transported him into a faraway world that made him feel prosperous, as though his life had prospects. Just looking at the photographs gave him the sense that there could be more to his existence than ploughing the earth throughout the endless cycle of the seasons. If he was sure of only one thing, it was that one day he would live there. He had no desire to live the rest of his life in poverty. As soon as his family was settled up at Campo Alto, he would leave them for the city.

The boys from Podervecchio had told him the Florentines were building now. Hospitals, train stations and enormous meat markets were under construction, and they needed bricklayers on site. Mario would go down to the valley of Florence and find his fortune. When it was time to go he would simply bid everyone goodbye and leave. No one could dissuade him. His father would try; in his typical dictatorial way he would tell Mario that he could not go. But Mario was not like the other country boys; he was an advanced thinker and would not spend his life 'honouring' his father's decisions when what that really meant was being dominated by him.

Mario was also hopeful that the Florentines would not be hostile towards a former farmer. Surely in their sophistication they would not show the same hate as did the townspeople here? When he stood tall by his mother's rabbits and ricotta at the marketplace in Stia, the people's dislike wafted towards him like an ill wind.

For now, his plans were secret. They had to be. His migration, which may as well have been to America for all the contact he would have with his family, would have dire consequences. His departure would leave only three girls and a nine-year-old boy to help their father. One less man on the land could mean ruin for the Bruni family. But he would not give up his dream of Florence. Mario slipped into a brooding silence.

The road to Podervecchio (Old Farm), was on the same back track that he and his father had followed a hundred times to reach the Stia markets. Podervecchio itself was situated about five kilometres below Poggio. In the sharp descent to reach it, the children hung on to the *treggia*'s sides and leant back as though riding a horse downhill. If the *treggia* had wheels the momentum gathered would have pushed the yoke off the oxen's necks and the cart would have crushed the animals from behind.

The land the Bruni children passed had undergone a dramatic colour change over the last few weeks. They were in the crisp, brittle brown months now, where everything they stepped on crackled. Shocks of burnt brown, orange and russet dominated the woods. Some trees had relinquished all their leaves to autumn; others hung on to their foliage while the colder air leached their colour.

As soon as they came to the cypress tree that marked the turn-off onto Podervecchio's track, Fiamma and Silvio jumped off the *treggia* and ran all the way to the farmhouse. They were excited, as shucking, or husking, the corn, then grating the dried kernels off the cob, was one of the farming calendar's social highlights. It was not as gruelling as bringing in the grain, as it had already been harvested and needed only to be shucked, grated and bagged. Most of their friends would be there because Podervecchio was one of the twenty-seven farms Poggio's owner possessed. The families that lived closer to each other worked to earn their corn together, especially the higher altitude families that could not grow their own. Corn, like olives and grapes, cannot grow above an altitude of six to seven hundred metres.

Maria and Anna stayed on the *treggia* till Mario pulled up alongside the house to let them off. The girls had been licking their fingertips and rubbing their eyebrows and eyelashes to remove dust from their faces. They shook out their headscarves and patted down their dresses, trying not to be too obvious with their grooming. There were boys here today, maybe potential husbands, so both girls took extra care to look pretty and neat. When they had nodded to each other that they were presentable, they collected the gifts – four pots of the family's tomato *conserva* – and slipped off the *treggia* in search of Giubbotto. He also managed Podervecchio and would pass on the Brunis' gift to Poggio's owner.

Mario could see that most of the other farmers had already arrived, as various mules and oxen were being led into the farm's barn. In the courtyard, men and boys called greetings to each other as they strode towards three mountains of corn ears, tossing still more on top. The corn had been harvested some time ago and had been hanging in bunches of twenty along the barn's ceiling and walls to dry. An old man with a knife sat on a chair slowly slashing the leaves that bound them together. Leading the oxen into the barn to take off their yoke and water them, Mario was spotted by Il Mangiatore (the Eater), the farmer who ran Podervecchio. He greeted Mario with a thunderous clap on the back and a bellow.

Il Mangiatore had ten sons, three daughters and a massive spread of land that included grapes, olives, wheat, barley, oats, chickpeas, beans, potatoes and most anything else that could sprout and be eaten. With his throng of big sons, he was considered a man blessed by God, even if his gluttony put him a little more on the questionable side of those permitted through the narrow gate into heaven. Il Mangiatore had a fondness for food and wine that had earnt him not only his nickname but a stomach the size of an oak barrel. It bobbed like a watermelon in water whenever he laughed, which was often.

Il Mangiatore's ten boys also loved to drink and did so, mostly to excess. It was here, to Podervecchio's barn, that Mario Bruni often came to *veglia*. The unmarried boys sat around on the hay, fetching the flasks as they needed them. Because Il Mangiatore drank a considerable amount himself, he failed to notice that certain shelves of wine disappeared. If he did see his stock dwindling he assumed that it had been bartered for sausages or fish, not spirited away by his sons and their friends.

Although Il Mangiatore had the biggest of all of Poggio's owner's farms, most of his yield went towards keeping fed his wife, his thirteen children, his mother, his father, an elderly unwed uncle, two daughters-in-law and three grandchildren. After he had given the farm's owner his gifts and paid him half of everything, Il Mangiatore and his wife were rarely left with cash for clothes, shoes or utensils. To counter this problem Il Mangiatore had one day come up with an ingenious plan that ultimately became one of Casentino's most famous quick-money plots. One evening, he paid his children not to have dinner, and then charged them for breakfast the next morning.

Apparently, after washing his hands, neatly combing his mutton chops and olive-oiling his hair flat, the big man stood obstructing the dinner table when his thirteen children and their wives crashed in for their evening meal.

'Tonight, my children,' he yelled over the chatter, 'you can choose to have either dinner or money.'

The children looked at each other as though their father had gone mad – who would choose food over money? Having had so little cash in the family and never in their own hands, all the children chose the coin, as their father had guessed they would.

'The money! The money!' they cried.

Il Mangiatore then slipped them some lira, and they all happily wandered off to bed, discussing what they'd spend their newfound wealth on. The next morning they could smell the steaming chestnut polenta drizzled with pork fat and chunks of bacon from their bedrooms. When they charged down the stairs for breakfast, their stomachs rumbling with hunger, they found their father before the breakfast table with his arms folded.

'There's a small charge for breakfast this morning,' he said to them all as they crowded around.

Their mouths dropped to their feet, but they put their hands into their pockets or ducked upstairs to their hidey-holes and retrieved their payment for going hungry the night before. Il Mangiatore and his wife saved on one meal that week and it was said they bought boots with the proceeds.

On corn-husking day Il Mangiatore was in his element. He loved having lots of friends over and looked forward to everyone sitting around outside, laughing and telling jokes while they worked. He was proud of his home and imagined it as the best *casa colonica* (Tuscan farmhouse) in the area. An imposing two-floor establishment, with four rooms upstairs and four downstairs, it lent itself well to outdoor work and socialising. To reach his front door one had to pass through the *aia* onto a set of stone stairs that were worn down by a million treads. It led up to a marvellous terrace with a view of his fields and into his enormous kitchen. The veranda itself was special because it had three columns with arches that granted the house the air of a *casa signorile* (a refined home for wealthy people). Under the stairs was another graceful arch that led into an open-air working area, all of it paved with giant grey flagstones, laid like a castle's many hundreds of years ago. The working area led down into cellars that were as cool as a forest on a spring night. Here he fermented his wine, stored his olive oil and cheese. In his two-storey barn he kept his animals below and his grains and feeds up high on the mezzanine level.

After welcoming the families while they settled their animals, Il Mangiatore walked from the barn to the courtyard. He saw that Maria and Anna Bruni were at the foot of the stairs to the house, handing over gifts to Giubbotto. Though the *conserva* was not sold for profit, it was still considered farm produce so therefore had to be shared, along with vegetables and eggs, with the farm's owners. A wide grin spread over Il Mangiatore's face when he saw what the *fattore* was wearing: a tan linen jacket that was far too fancy for a day grating corn. The girls bobbed a half-hearted curtsy to their manager and went to settle themselves with the other women and children in the circle that was forming around the corn.

'Only the sun has more light than you, dear Maria,' greeted Il Mangiatore as he walked towards the group. 'And you, little Anna! My, my! Growing up so fast. A young woman now, I see.'

'*Buon giorno*, Signore,' the girls said in unison.

'How's the chestnut man? I hear he's hired help for himself this year. He must have tricks, your father. Tell me what they are,' Il Mangiatore teased.

The girls laughed and shyly shook their heads. Fiamma and Silvio ran up to join them, as it appeared work would soon be underway.

'I'll find out through these two then, even if I have to grate it out of them with the corn. How does your father fill his chestnut baskets? Like the loaves and the fishes, that man. One tree, one hundred baskets of chestnuts.'

The children giggled while Il Mangiatore made a pleading gesture to heaven and shrugged, his great girth heaving with the movement; then he left them for the storage area under the house to collect more graters. He had known the Brunis for many years and liked their young ones. In his opinion Artemio was a very good farmer. Ambitious, though: one could read the determination in the lines of his face. He thought Artemio would want to be careful with that. A lot of men did not like aspiration. It challenged their sense of order and made them feel inadequate, especially if that aspiration turned into money. No one liked to hear another man's pocket jingling louder than his.

Mario appeared to have inherited his father's resoluteness. They looked so alike too. Il Mangiatore had mistaken son for father often at the markets. Neither man ever smiled, though Artemio was likeable, as one could understand him. It was difficult to grow fond of Mario, however. Perhaps he'd taken Primo's death hard. Il Mangiatore had heard that the Brunis were moving to Campo Alto and he thought if anyone could make a success of that rocky mountaintop farm, Artemio and Mario could. Personally, he would not even consider taking over his own brother's farm. It wouldn't feel right, as if he himself had had a hand in kicking him off his land. Artemio had an odd knack with those chestnuts, though. Time would tell how he fared without them.

When Il Mangiatore returned to the corn, some women had already started shucking. Within minutes they were all discarding the shanks and putting the silks into a pile for the mattresses. The rustling roughness of the dried leaves as they were ripped off sounded like a bustling waterfall. Il Mangiatore's elderly parents and uncle, their faces the colour and texture of cork, helped too. They kept their eyes on their grandchildren, speaking to them in the words reserved especially for children. '*Cecce!*' instead of *sedere* for 'sit down'. '*Nene!*' instead of *bere* for 'drink'. '*Mima!*' instead of *bambina* for 'baby girl'.

The first job was to untie the bunches of corn before passing the ears along to be peeled. The girls adjusted their long skirts under their bottoms for comfort as they reached forward for ear after ear. Some lowered their eyes meekly and were hard to engage in conversation. Others had eyes like hungry cats, alert to any sign of interest thrown their way and devouring it when it was. This was one of the few opportunities for the mountain boys and girls to make eyes at each other, perhaps even have a word on their own. The boys worked well, pulling the shanks off quickly, eager to show off their skill. Nonchalantly, they had positioned themselves alongside the signorina that for them shined the brightest.

Their mothers on the opposite side of the circle never missed a glance. No potential romance escaped their attention. They subtly raised their eyebrows at each other, leaving any potentially embarrassing comment till *veglia*, when every gesture, no matter how insignificant, would be dissected and judged.

Good-natured humour flowed with their work. The woman who'd had a baby every year accepted with a maternal smile the digs at her gaffe twelve months ago. Someone had said teasingly to her, 'Was it a boy?' and she'd responded, 'You must have the sight! How did you know I'd had another baby?' The group had roared with laughter as apparently she was the only one who did not realise that she had a baby every year. She was only twenty-nine and already a mother of nine. The census man had come through her village several years earlier. Intially unable to remember the birth date of one of her children, she'd eventually said to him, 'Now I recall: Little Giacomino was born on Stia's market day! A Tuesday! *Si, si*, write down Tuesday.' The group laughed at these jokes, even though they'd heard them all before.

Il Mangiatore presided over the rustling and ripping of the leaves with a song to go with the order of the harvests that he had composed himself. He sang loudly in a deep bass:

First your grain, then your corn,
Grapes for wine and your olives for your oil.
Then find your tools and a warm blaze
For it's inside you'll stay, to rest from your toil.

Maria laughed along with the others, but felt extremely self-conscious. The skin up the back of her neck had begun to crawl and it frightened her. There was a new mother shucking today and she had a very fetching daughter by her side. They were part of a family that had recently taken on one of the owner's farms near Romena Castle. The matron's glance kept returning to Maria's face. She'd throw her encouraging expressions, smile and nod at her. But it was a veil; there was coldness there. The daughter was unusually blonde. She held herself in a way that told Maria she was accustomed always to being the prettiest girl in the group. But there was no innocence in her eyes. It was as if she were adding everyone up to see who fell into what category. When Giubbotto slouched over to the group the girl sat up straighter and appeared merry. Her smile faded as she watched Giubbotto's back when he passed her and went to Maria. Always, he stopped behind Maria, pausing longer there than anywhere else. Maria felt his presence like a blacksmith's fire blazing at her shoulder. The pretty girl watched all of this and weighed it up like a set of scales.

'True beauty is a rare thing, but we seem to have been given more than our fair share. Another beauty to add to our Maria, eh?' chuckled Il Mangiatore as he waved his hand towards the pretty new girl.

'You two are going to give Stia a reputation for good-looking women,' someone else called.

'And all the boys from Tuscany will come here looking for a bride,' added another voice.

'Won't they be disappointed when they see you!' yet another voice teased.

'My daughter was named the flower of our village before we moved to Romena,' responded the girl's mother, raising her voice over the banter.

'Ah, but no one can compare with our Angel. She is our pride.' Il Mangiatore smiled indulgently.

Mother and daughter looked at each other, then continued their work.

Maria's hand crept up to her neck. She traced the outline of her mother's rosary beads with her fingertips. The beads had been put around her neck today with a special blessing to keep her safe. Maria had been allowed to visit Podervecchio only because her family needed the portion of corn she would earn.

Anna whispered beside her, 'Pull them out.' As the group focused its attention elsewhere, Maria coaxed the string of beads out. Light as a feather, the olive pips had been bleached to a sandy-grey colour. She let the wooden crucifix hang down between her breasts. Jesus had more power to fight the evil of envy when out in the open.

By noon the shanks and silks had been sorted so the group began to *raspare* the corn. With graters that came up to their knees, everyone rubbed till the dried kernels popped off their cobs like kicked pebbles rat-ta-tat-tatting along a gravel road.

Giubbotto kept his eye on the group from a distance. He pulled his hands out of his pockets to scratch at his neck and followed Il Mangiatore on his quests for water or bags. He'd had farmers steal corn before and had not hesitated to call for the *carabinieri* – military police. One family had shoved some ears into a sack and hidden the sack in their hay. He'd had a feeling they'd try to dupe him and had remained vigilant. The third man ransacked the barn and, upon discovering the sack of corn ears, had been immediately despatched to Stia to alert the *carabinieri*. Giubbotto had the family finish their work and stayed with them until the police arrived. They'd denied secreting the bag away but he'd kept his head and calmly explained to the police how only they could have bagged up the corn, probably straight after the harvest, way before shucking, when he and his guards had left for the day. The farmer was charged with stealing produce from his owner – *raspollare* – and was thrown off the land that night. Giubbotto had watched with satisfaction as the family packed their belongings onto a borrowed *treggia* and drove into town in the moonlight. He'd heard they'd moved in with cousins. On the odd occasion he saw that same family, creeping about from house to house, begging for bread. He'd done his best to black-ban them from ever working again. They'd never be given another farm; they were thieves and rightly branded so, *pigionali* (renters) till their children grew up and lost their parents' stigma.

When the sun was high in the sky, Il Mangiatore's wife and her daughters-in-law set up a table in the shade cast by the rafters of the house. They covered the table with floral cloths and brought trays and pots of food down the stairs from the kitchen. When satisfied that all was perfectly arranged, the signora banged a wooden spoon against a lid and called, '*Si mangia!*' The men rose immediately to their feet but stood back respectfully to allow Giubbotto to take first place in the queue that would soon form in front of the signora's table. There were far too many people to seat, so everyone was expected to collect their food before finding a place to sit on the ground.

Giubbotto and his guard strolled forward and took their plates, piled high with *tortelli di patate* and a generous dollop of sauce. Within seconds the courtyard began to exhale the sauce's aroma and the men started to call out, '*Che bontà oggi!* What goodness for us today!' A surly woman who brooked no fuss, the signora accepted the compliments with a wave of her hand, even though it had taken her days to prepare this feast.

First she had made the pasta – yards and yards of it had stretched like a drying roll of hemp across the kitchen chairs and larder shelves. To make the *tortellis'* filling, the signora had smothered more than a dozen bulbs of finely diced garlic with olive oil over a gentle flame in her fireplace. She had then boiled kilos of potatoes till tender, peeled them and passed them through a sieve so that they became as smooth as velvet. She mixed the garlic and several containers of her tomato *conserva* through the potatoes, with lots of salt. When it was dense and tasty enough to fill the pasta, she spent a day slicing and folding the *tortellis* into neat matchbox-size squares. For the sauce, she ejected many pork sausages out of their skins and mushed them up into a large terracotta pot with oil and lots of chopped onions. If asked, she would have said that the secret to her sauce was to let the onions and sausage sizzle long and well over a slow fire, adding drizzles of water so that nothing dried out to become brown and hard. After stirring through another substantial amount of *conserva*, she put the sauce, with more water, into the coals of her fire to slow roast and thicken for a few hours.

For the second course, everyone took their plates back for artichokes stewed in olive oil, lemon juice, bay leaves, parsley, wild herbs and a dash of water. The artichokes were paired with a thick slice of bread.

With full bellies and contented smiles, the farmers finally exchanged their dishes for an apple or two. They sat in groups, the young girls in one, munching, murmuring and looking furtively at the eligible young boys, who stood, horsing around. The men and women, too, sat in separate circles, each in conversation about what interested them, enjoying the peace before the afternoon session began.

After half an hour Il Mangiatore struggled heavily to his

feet and said, 'Come on, let's start again.' There still remained much work to be done. The woody cores of the corn ears lay in heaps around the *aia*, along with piles of leaves as tall as a man. Everybody rose and took their grating positions once again.

When the sun was low behind the mountains above Podervecchio, the *aia* looked neater; only the kernels were left in organised mounds. Silvio held a hessian bag open for Mario as he shovelled the corn into a sack. Maria stood beside them twisting twine around the sacks to secure them. Fiamma and Anna dragged them over to a growing wall that looked like sandbags ready to dam a flood.

'Mario, I want a word with you,' beckoned Giubbotto from the bottom of the stairs to the house. Mario rested his shovel and told Silvio to help the girls move the sacks to the *treggias* that would soon be loaded for the mill. Giubbotto waited for Mario, then turned to lead him behind the house for what would obviously be a private talk. With every step Mario felt his muscles tense into a guarded readiness. When Giubbotto called someone for a one-on-one talk, it never boded well. The two men passed the arch under the house where Il Mangiatore stored his olive oil, wine and tools. When Giubbotto reached the grass off the cobblestones, he turned to face Mario.

'This is not enough *conserva*,' he said roughly, pointing to the four pot-belly jars that the girls had given him earlier. He had placed them in a line on the ground so that they looked like rejects out in the backyard of a shop.

'Your owner will not be happy. Your mother should be more generous to her masters. Tell your father to bring more on Tuesday to the markets. I'll pick them up there.'

Mario hated the word 'master' – *padrone*. Giubbotto said

it as if the Brunis were selfish swindlers intent on cheating a benevolent employer, when all their *padrone* did was increase their hunger while living in a villa with a full larder. Mario wanted to say, 'We are not thieves and if you take more *conserva* there will be nothing left for my family.' But he did not. He checked himself and nodded, knowing all along that Giubbotto wanted the *conserva* for himself. Four pots were not enough for *him* and their master. But he could not accuse his manager of this or speak back to him in any way. Giubbotto had all the power. With a few carefully chosen phrases he could have the Brunis ordered off their land. They'd starve while waiting for Campo Alto to be vacated. Mario started to turn back to the others.

'You know,' Giubbotto went on, 'I could make your life quite difficult. You do realise that, don't you, Mario?'

Mario stopped and stared at his manager. He did not know what Giubbotto was angling at.

'A word here, a word there. I know some things about your father that could destroy him.'

Mario felt his skin tighten.

'Don't misunderstand me. I'm not threatening you. Just making a suggestion. *Mi capisci?*'

Mario understood him, all right. He knew this language. Suggestion was another word for bribe.

'What do you want, Mr Farm Manager?'

'I can see you've got no hairs on your tongue – that is, you always tell the truth. And as the oldest son of your family now, I imagine your word would have some sway with your father.'

Mario did not think anyone's word could influence his father's views. Still, he stayed quiet. His throat was constricting tighter and tighter. He tried to swallow the suffocating feeling of anger and frustration that had begun to swell in his neck. Giubbotto did not notice.

'It's your influence I want, Mario. But before I go on, let me say that it's a matter of an elder tree I saw being removed from state land.'

Mario had seen the elder tree that Giubbotto was referring to. It was hidden among the light shifts of material used to strain the ricotta. By winter the tree would be shoes for his little brothers and sisters.

'The forest guards need know nothing.' Here Giubbotto slowed and appeared to become somewhat unsure of himself. His eyes darted behind him as he looked over his shoulder and rubbed at his rolled scarf. He plunged on. 'Your sister is a remarkable woman.'

Mario let out an involuntary gasp.

'I know, I know,' Giubbotto said, holding his hand up and humbly hanging his head. 'A man of my stature taking an interest in a farmer's daughter.' He took a breath and puffed out his chest. 'Put a word, a favourable word, into your father's ear about me. Let him know I am interested in making Maria my bride. I'm sure then that we will hear nothing from the forest guards, eh?'

But Mario could no longer hear him for the noise like static that rushed through his ears. How dare he think that his sister was a piece of meat that could be won with a bribe? Demanding more *conserva* for himself was one matter, but demanding a woman?

When Mario went for Giubbotto his throat released a gurgle that grew into a strangled roar. His first punch hit him straight across the left cheek so that Giubbotto's head snapped to the side. The second came immediately after and smashed into his jaw. The blows blurred into a barrage as

Giubbotto snorted with shock and tried to protect his face with his arms.

It did not take Mario long to disconnect from his surroundings; every blow released some pent-up feeling of injustice against him, committed by a snide manager, a superior villager, a despotic father. Mario hated his life and when his fists slammed into Giubbotto, it numbed his voiceless pain.

Maria's skirt swept silently across the stones beside the house as she searched for Mario. In the late-afternoon sunlight her face was ethereal. The wind lifted the hair around her forehead; her headscarf had come loose. Anxiously she pushed back the stray strands and glanced about her for her brother and their manager. She'd been the only one to notice the alarmingly guttural sound that came from behind Il Mangiatore's house.

When she found them, Giubbotto was on the ground, covered in blood. Mario was mechanically raising his fists and bringing them down. When she screamed at him to stop, he kept on swinging. She knew he could not hear her. She'd seen him like this before. Mario's face was closed, his eyes were hooded. The vein in his temple throbbed. She could smell his fury from where she stood; it rose off his body with a sickly, tangy odour.

When others came running, Giubbotto was beside the jars he'd so neatly lined up earlier, on his side in the foetal position. As they pulled Mario off him, he opened his eyes and fixed Maria with a stare unlike anything she'd ever seen. It searched her, accused her, lusted after her. In one short gaze, Giubbotto said it all and she understood that this beating was because of her. She knew it because of his lingering looks and pauses behind her back. In his way he'd been telling her all along that he wanted her but she had never understood.

When Mario saw Maria he screamed, 'Sister! You stay away from him!' Then he snarled at Giubotto, 'Touch her and you will die.'

The farmers looked at Maria and suddenly they, too, understood the reason for this fracas. They knew it because these were the rules in the country. The loveliest girls always went to the man of the highest stature: the manager, the farm guard, the third man, the forest guard, the policeman. They had the pick of the crop. How could they have doubted that their angel, Maria, would be sought by one of them?

Someone helped Giubbotto to his feet. He shook them off and wiped his bloodied forehead with the crook of his arm. With his thumb and forefinger he felt his nose. Blood dripped onto the palm of his hand. Giubbotto looked at it thoughtfully while everyone stood back and watched. Then he looked up at Mario.

'*Te ne pentirai.* You will regret this.'

❦

The *treggia* trundled onto Poggio's track well after sundown. At the sound of the dogs barking, Bruna took a sleepy baby Pasquale off her breast and carried him up to bed. Ottavia and Artemio were asleep. Her spinach and bean soup was ready to ladle into dishes for the returning children. A basin of water, soap and clean towels for their hands lay on the sink. They would return tired, hungry and dirty after a day of corn harvesting at Podervecchio.

Bruna patted the baby into position alongside Artemio and came down the stairs in time to see Maria come into the kitchen, leaning heavily against Mario. Bruna paused, stone still.

'She has a fever,' Mario said, pushing his sister past his mother up the stairs. 'I'll take her to her room.'

As quick as an old woman passing a cemetery, Bruna crossed herself. 'Mary, Holy Mother of God, grant us peace,' she breathed.

Anna and Fiamma fumbled in the front door with sacks of corn shanks over their shoulders. Bruna went for the jug of water and gathered up a clean towel.

'The fever started just as we left Il Mangiatore's,' offered Anna quietly.

'But why? Who was there? Did someone do something to her?' Bruna was heading quickly back up the stairs, but she paused to look closely at the girls. They appeared meek, as though some sin had been committed.

'Should I wake your father?'

The girls nodded their heads.

'Should I worry?'

Once again, they nodded.

Bruna bathed Maria's hands and face, then saw her off into a fitful sleep. She heard the girls help themselves to the soup and Mario go off to the barn to sort the oxen after Silvio came in with the last bags of corn leaves. Only then did she wake Artemio.

She sat up with her husband and eldest living son, talking till late. As they discussed the situation, Artemio said that given the circumstances, he might have been tempted to react in the same way. But he would never have lost control of himself so thoroughly. Artemio lectured his son on violence, saying no good ever came from it, and now the Bruni family faced a terrible predicament because of it. Mario's lack of restraint had sealed Maria's fate in a way no threat over a stolen tree ever could.

If Giubbotto really wanted Maria, he could use this thrashing as a lever. He could say to the Brunis, 'I'll go to the *cara-*

binieri and have Mario incarcerated unless you give me Maria's hand.' If Artemio refused, Giubbotto could have both Mario and Artemio, thanks to the elder tree, arrested. The family would lose their men and ruin awaited their move to Campo Alto. That would leave Artemio with no choice; he would have to let Maria go to Giubbotto. It was no use thinking that the police might believe Mario's story – that he bashed Giubbotto in defence against corruption. They would side with Giubbotto, the most influential complainant.

The trio talked in circles until Artemio decided that all they could do was wait. Giubbotto would eventually come. The question was, would he come alone or with the police? If he brought the police, Mario would be arrested and Maria might go free. If he came alone, still intent on his bribes and Maria, she would be condemned to a loveless marriage and Mario would go free.

Before the stars in the pitch sky dissolved into a curtain of pink and orange, Bruna roused herself to check on her daughter. She found Maria's cheeks aflame, her eyes swollen and her fever raging. Her breathing came in quick, short breaths and she refused Bruna's suggestion of water. Bruna padded downstairs in her thick socks anyway, to stir up the fire and make her some chamomile tea. When the brew cooled, she went back up the stairs to make Maria sip a little from a glass.

Bruna took out Maria's braids and ran her fingers through he daughter's hair. It was long, past her bottom, and as dark as the night that had just passed. Bruna looked critically at her daughter. Her eyebrows were thin, as though sketched on with ink. She had full lips or, as her sisters would say, meaty lips, and a heart-shaped face. She was slight, like Artemio, not big-boned like Bruna, Anna and Fiamma. Sometimes even Bruna, accustomed as she was to her children's spectacular eyes, was taken aback by how captivating was her daughter's face.

Looking past her beauty and into her soul, Bruna could see a timid child who suffered for her good looks. She hummed Maria a mournful ballad about a maiden's lost love while she replaited her hair. Anna, Fiamma and Ottavia slept on, undisturbed by their mother's gentle ministering.

When dawn distilled into the deep blue of early morning, Bruna went back down to the kitchen. She could not cast from her mind the thought that Maria's fever would not pass. It was a chest infection, she was sure of it. Maybe Maria had consumption, as Primo had, and would be taken from her. Perhaps she had been cursed. Perhaps someone, somewhere, had made an effigy of her child out of candle wax and straw and was torturing it. Her fever would cripple her for years, coming and going at the malevolent spirit's whim.

Bruna marked time by touching things, dragging her fingertips along the surfaces of the table and shelves as though checking for dust. She dug her fingernails into the crevices of the stone sink, but did not excavate the dirt, as she could not see it for her worry. The wicker trays that held the drying *porcini* mushrooms near the grate became like guitar strings as she strummed and picked at them.

She could wait no longer; grabbing her shawl and boots, she headed out the door for Signora Mazzetti's. Her old friend was the only one who could properly advise on Maria.

After a flurry of knocks, brief kisses and explanations, the wise woman collected some of her remedies and donned her shawl. Pulling it low over her face, her back hunched more than ever from concern and purposefulness, she hastened back up the road with Bruna.

Once inside the house, Signora Mazzetti went up the stairs, telling Bruna to bring up a bowl of water immediately. She shooed the younger girls out of their bed and down to breakfast with a backwards call: 'Take baby Pasquale with you too.' At the foot of Maria's bed, she spread open the square of material that held her equipment: a wooden cone, a small vial of blessed Camaldoli monk oil, a fig leaf and two pieces of wood tied together with a tatty piece of string.

A fan of rays that came through the gaps in the drawn shutters dimly lit the room. The walls were grey, adorned only by last year's Palm Sunday olive twigs that were twisted into a crucifix above the bed. Along with the slight smell of Ottavia's urine from the mattress was the smell of unvarnished wood and children's nighttime breath. In the corner, like ghostly apparitions, the sacks of fresh corn leaves lay waiting.

Settling herself at Maria's side, Signora Mazzetti rested her hands for about thirty seconds over the girl's head, chest, stomach, legs and feet in turn. It seemed to Bruna that she was drawing out the girl's temperature with her open palms.

'The heat's coming from her head,' Signora Mazzetti reported. She took the wooden cone and put it to her ear, listening to Maria's chest. 'No rattles,' she said.

'Praise be to the Madonna!' Bruna whispered.

'No swelling,' continued Signora Mazzetti as she laid her hands against either side of Maria's neck, feeling under her ears. 'You have no sore throat, no headache or pains?'

Maria shook her head. Signora Mazzetti sat back a little and stared at the girl's face. She looked pallid and listless, but there was something else. It took Signora Mazzetti a while to put her finger on it, but eventually it came to her. Melancholy. More than anything, Maria looked sad.

'I can detect no sickness,' determined the elderly woman. 'Now give me the water,' she ordered. Putting the vial of oil into Maria's hand, Signora Mazzetti told Maria to pour the contents into the water.

'The oil is not separating, it's pooling together.'

'Blessed thanks to Mary!' Bruna exclaimed.

'*Sì*, no demons. On the way here, you mentioned that Anna had suggested that a new mother and daughter from Romena Castle may have cast Maria the evil eye. The holy oil tells me they have not. But you must be alert! Come downstairs and I will tell you how to recognise the signs of Satan, and you must tell me what happened in the hours before Maria's fever.'

Breathing out an indistinct chant, Signora Mazzetti put the fig leaf in the bowl of water and oil. Giving it to Bruna, she told her to place it under the sickbed. With reverence she picked up the pieces of wood and string and passed them to Maria.

'Hold on to this. It is old coffin wood, an amulet against the grave. It will help your spirit fight against death and its dominion.' She patted Maria's head and cheek, then turned to pack up her belongings.

The two women went down the stairs, their footsteps reverberating around the vacated house, which had already taken on the hushed, dejected air of an infirmary. They sat on chairs in front of the fire and Bruna told Signora Mazzetti what Maria had witnessed at Podervecchio.

Signora Mazzetti very quickly diagnosed *le paure* – a bad fright – a very normal response to shock. Heavens, she said, the child had suffered a trauma; of course her body would collapse into feverish agitation. She leant over and squeezed

Bruna's knee and said she was sure her beautiful daughter was not ill from a disease and that her fever would pass. But till then, and just to be safe from a curse by Giubbotto or the Romena women, she instructed her friend on the devil's presence.

Beware of sounds: if the dogs, sheep or oxen appeared unusually excited or there were unexplained noises in the house. Watch for clumps of soot falling from the chimney, things disappearing, the explosion of a flask, an owl's call from outside Maria's window at sunset or sunrise. All these could mean the powers of darkness were at work.

Signora Mazzetti took Bruna's salt urn, blessed it, and then scattered the salt around the bottom of the stairs to hinder Satan's passage. She promised to return in the evening with a tonic and advised Bruna to bathe Maria's brow with a cold cloth.

Walking Signora Mazzetti to the door, Bruna asked suddenly, 'Did you know why they call Mario "Trincia"?'

Signora Mazzetti took both Bruna's hands and squeezed them. 'I had a fair idea, yes.'

Bruna shook her head wearily. 'Isn't there something we can do for him?'

'I can only help those who want me to.'

'Of course.' The women hugged each other. Signora Mazzetti started to walk through the doorway but stopped and turned back to Bruna. 'If there's no change in two days, we'll gather the women.'

'Yes! We'll go to the Madonna and ask her for a blessing!'

Bruna returned to the kitchen feeling a little better. Now that there was a plan to aid Maria, and she'd been diagnosed, the knots of worry began to untangle. However, in their place a new one quickly formed. While nursing Maria the reason for Mario's nickname had dawned on Bruna, with heart-crushing clarity. Trincia. To her ears the word itself sounded sharp. To cut, slice, split. He'd been given that name because he'd attacked before.

Thinking it through now, she realised that she'd suspected for some time that something was not quite right with Mario. A mother always sees her children's vices, but if they are too unpleasant, she will deny them, or ignore them. Mother-love bolted maternal hearts shut against the faults of children, especially sons, she thought.

Bruna thought, too, of Artemio's chestnut trees. He had a saying about them: a crooked tree is malleable only when young. The quirk in a sapling's stem can always be straightened out with some cord and a steadfast stick. But if the tree is left unattended as it grows, its bent trunk becomes impossible to fix. It will snap if forced. Just like babies with their leg bindings, it had to be set right when young. It was too late for Mario, he had taken his shape and nothing would change him.

Bruna picked up a walnut and rubbed its corrugated shell. She remembered one *veglia* when a travelling storyteller had come to their house with an accordion. The whole family had crammed around the hearth to listen, rapt, to his stories and fables of kings and queens from long ago. Then they'd danced to his music, Artemio too, in circles of laughter, tripping over each other's feet, the girls clutching their stomachs from their giggles. Primo had been alive then, it was the year before he was taken. A handsome eighteen year old, he'd bowed low and pretended he was a squire when he'd extended his hand to her blossoming Maria, requesting the next jig. It had been one of the happiest moments of her life, seeing her whole family united in love and fun. But in the shadows was Mario. Bruna remembered that he had been trying to grow a moustache but that, as he was only sixteen years old, it looked more like a splindly weed. He had not joined in, though she'd tried to cajole him by calling his name, beckoning to him with her finger. He had stayed aloof all that evening. She had wondered what was wrong with him, but had brushed her apprehension away, deciding that his habitual detachment was exacerbated by his impatience to be an adult. She had told herself that he was a fine boy because he was such a hard worker, so able and quiet. But by thrashing Giubbotto he had confirmed her worst fears. Her baby had not grown into a good man.

Artemio's response to the family's quandary was to hide himself in his *seccatoio* – the chestnut drying house. The smell of the sweet smoke that impregnated the charred stone walls soothed him. The time was coming when the branches that rested on the wooden beams halfway up the *seccatoio* would be full of fat brown chestnuts. He felt enormously comforted by this thought. Bruna nurtured the home and the children, but this was where he was needed, right here, sweeping up the ash from last year's fire, caring for his chestnuts.

He'd finished the previous evening's discussions with Mario with an order to do the worst job of the year: carry all the human and animal excrement from the manure pit behind the house to the fields, without any help from his brother or sisters. He was angry with his son and deeply disappointed. Artemio felt that a lengthy, repellent occupation was just what the boy deserved for placing his family in such dreadful circumstances.

Artemio put thoughts of his troubled son from his mind. He swept up the charred skins from last year's chestnuts into a neat, waist-high heap up against the wall. Dousings of those would keep this year's flames low and measured. Once the floor was tidied, Artemio went outside and up to the front window of the drying house. From there, he could reach in to pull out the branches that lay like a grille across the beams. About the width of a man's wrist, the sturdy sticks had to be reset neatly side by side, each at the right distance from the other, not so far apart that the chestnuts fell through and not so close together that the fire's heat could not penetrate.

This was the last time he would clean out his *seccatoio*, which gave him conflicting emotions. It had served him well and he had grown very fond of it. Next year, for the first time in his life, he would not spend October, November and December devoted to the cultivation of chestnuts. A feeling of loss waved over him. The thought of being without his chestnuts made his confidence desert him.

Even if Campo Alto did have a drying house, it would not have compared favourably with Poggio's. This one was only three steps away from his front door. Many people had their drying houses in the woods, near their chestnuts, so that they did not have far to carry them. Convenient in theory, but difficult when it came to checking the fire that had to burn constantly beneath the nuts.

Most of Tuscany's *seccatoios* looked like tiny houses or mini Swiss chalets. Artemio's looked more like a rustic chapel in miniature. It had a pointed roof over a jumble of stones that looked higgledy-piggledy but were actually laid in perfect symmetry. From the front, it appeared only two metres tall, with a knee-high window. However, inside it was cut into the earth, where the land dropped away, and so the room was actually about six metres high. A door from the rear gave internal access. Two windows, the size of a hand span in width and an arm in length, let the smoke circulate and escape from the *seccatoio*'s side walls.

In Artemio's mind, this drying house was perfect. When he needed to stoke the flames that huddled on the floor with a large piece of slate over the top of them to stop the sparks from setting the branches above alight, Artemio came in through the door. When the chestnuts had to be distributed upon the branches, he opened the knee-high window at the front and reached in. Artemio moved into his drying house for the month of November. Many men did. They slept on truckle beds under the rising plume of smoke that hovered halfway up the walls.

In a few weeks, maybe sooner, thousands of kilos of chestnuts would fall. Once they'd dried and shrivelled to a quarter of their size, they'd be peeled, and Artemio would take them to the mill to be ground into flour. He would then sell the chestnut flour to a merchant.

Artemio felt a twinge of excitement in his stomach. Last year's production had been a little more than half of this year's projection and it had padded Bruna's pocket quite nicely. He wasn't sure exactly how much money she had tucked away in her skirt now, but after this year's deliverance he was sure to be closer to buying his own land. Perhaps he could purchase an acre without a house, buy a home later when he had more cash. It was common to own an acre here and an acre there. His neighbour, Il Rosso, along with his brothers and sisters, had inherited his land. By the time the inheritance was distributed among all the siblings, Il Rosso's land was so broken up his wheatfield was next to Poggio's but he ran his sheep several kilometres away. And everyone knew that he had only had one son so that the family land would not be split any further.

Artemio mulled over the curious force that seemed to propel him. Though his friends wanted their own land, they had stopped working hard to save for it. Botte, Culino, Boccacia – they dragged an air of resignation behind them like sluggish shadows. He did not understand why they had given up on their dreams. His own need to achieve was urgent. Whatever task was at hand absorbed him till it was finished, only to be replaced immediately by another job that was no less important than the last, or the next. This cycle pushed him blindly forward from season to season towards the hope of a better life, like a blinkered carriage horse, forbidden distraction from left or right.

If he owned only a single hectare of land, it would raise him above the vast mass of rack-renting rural Italian peasants. Pray God that the Holy Mary would help him take that first step. Indeed, it would need nothing short of a miracle for him to rise above the *mezzadria* system – a small section of land that was not big enough to provide proper food or savings because half of everything produced was given to your owner, who could fire you for no reason and with no notice; farm contracts that held no written rules about seasonal gifts, apart from at Christmas and Easter, and on those two feast days a *mezzadro* had to go before his manager's *scrittoio* (desk) to have his eggs counted and fowls weighed.

He remembered the woman who had farmed the Romena Castle land before the new family. She had gone to the *scrittoio* and had her chickens weighed last Christmas. They were four hundred grams below the requested gift weight, whereas the farmer before her had been half a kilo over the contract weight. Giubbotto had told her to pay the shortfall the following Christmas.

'But the other farmer, the one with the extra half-kilo on his chickens, will you make him pay less next Christmas?'

Giubbotto had screamed at her to shut up, called her an impudent witch and told her to pack her family's belongings. The woman did not sleep another night in the Romena Castle house that had been hers for twenty-two years.

There was another manager in Casentino who was no better than Giubbotto. To make the family he managed work harder, he'd taken the fireplace out of the wall in the kitchen and had it put under the staircase. In that position, the mantle and chimney gave off no heat. To stay warm the family was forced to go out into the fields to work. To achieve his owner's quota for that farm, the manager had simply removed any temptation to stay inside and sit around a cosy fire.

As he settled his branches into place, Artemio's plan became clearer. The sale of this year's chestnut harvest would fund the purchase of his first tiny parcel of land. The profits from Campo Alto might just provide the rest.

***

As promised, Signora Mazzetti returned to Poggio on the fourth morning of Maria's fever, as there had been no change in the girl's condition. Behind Signora Mazzetti at the front door were Assunta, Bona, Giuseppa and Angelina – four of the women who lived a few kilometres beyond the Ospita's pastures and shared the church of Il Villaggio.

The group passed Bruna a handkerchief that held a few coins, all that the women were able to offer God in exchange for Maria's good health. Bruna felt tears in her eyes as she stepped away from her house and the others folded her into their midst. She had found herself collecting money and prayers for these women, in just the same way as they were doing for her now, all her adult life. It was the way of country life that the sorrows of one dwelt in the hearts of all. One person's troubles were everyone's troubles: when a husband fell from a chestnut tree, when a daughter went into early labour, when a son's cough turned into consumption. These were tragedies that were shared, made public knowledge through the church bells that chimed in a different rhythm, letting everyone know that the priest was at a sickbed with the host and the holy oil. In the fields, they all heard the bells and every head bowed in prayer.

The women walked in companionable silence, in grey, black or brown crocheted shawls that had their tasselled ends tucked into their waistbands so that the wool stayed out of their work. Everyone's head was covered by a faded scarf. It was a cold day, with tightly crammed dark clouds that distorted the colours around them.

The pilgrimage stopped at a further seven doors, all the homes that were clustered around Il Villaggio church. Tosca, Il Rosso's wife, said she could not join the group. Neither her son nor her husband would collect the water and they had run out. Men never fetched the water from the stream. It was below them and they would have been ashamed to be seen with a bucket in their hands. The women understood and moved on.

Argenta came to her door with rags tied to her feet, to buff the wood as she walked. She had her baby in a sling and another two holding on to each leg and no, she said, she had no one to leave them with and no spare coins. She promised to pray for Maria from home.

When each of the households was visited and a *soldino* (a copper portion of a lira) given, the group went to their church, La Pieve di Santa Maria Assunta. Chiselled into the stone lintel above its door was the inscription *Assumpta est Maria in Coelum* – Mary was taken into the sky.

Both Bona and Giuseppa leant their shoulders against the heavy wooden doors so that the women could file in one by one after a genuflexion, a sign of the cross over their chests and a kiss to their fingertips. The altar opposite the door was very simple. A stone table stood in front of an arch cut into the wall that framed a faded fresco of the angel Gabriel telling Mary that she was pregnant with God's son. Two brass candlesticks rested on a narrow gold tablecloth on the table. To the right of the altar was a small crucifix. To the left of the arch was a ceramic statue of Mary that was permanently hidden under a length of silk. The Madonna was too holy to be exposed; she could be seen only on special occasions, such as this one, when the women in the congregation petitioned her with money and prayers to intercede for them.

Signora Mazzetti took the position of the highly esteemed – beside the Madonna – while the women took their places in the front pews. Bruna approached the wooden box with the slot in the top that sat on a stool halfway up the aisle and slipped the coins in one by one. There was total concentration while the women listened to the light clink of the little *soldinis* as they landed in the offering chest.

At the ready, Signora Mazzetti stood by the covered Madonna, with her hand on its veil. When Bruna had taken her seat, Signora Mazzetti reverently slipped Mary's silk cover from her face. The women sighed, made another sign of the cross, shook their heads and clasped their hands in wonder. Assunta clapped her hands once, her face radiant. They were now in the presence of La Madonna.

She was their own personal mediator with God, and it was as though, when the statue was bared, her power were unleashed and there wasn't a wish in heaven she could not grant. When they were with their Holy Mary, none of their problems was insurmountable, all requests and supplications were heard and answered. Together, the women were a potent force, as they identified with the mother of God in a way they never could with Jesus or God. For Mary was a woman. She had blisters on her hands, went to the well for water, made the family's food, breastfed her babies, just like they did. But she was also more than a friend. La Madonna was their own special mother. She gave them all a love that was tender and selfless. After all, they would say, for whom do you call when you are lost? Your mamma! Who do you need when you are sick? Your mamma! La Madonna gave the women – the men too – her feminine love, and they revered her for it.

All heads bent in unison, to repeat prayers for the young and lovely Maria, who could so easily die from her fever. Angelina and Assunta slipped out their rosaries to click around their beads, their mouths moving soundlessly, every now and then a consonant escaping their lips. Others rocked back and forth in time with their chants. Signora Mazzetti sat bent down over her hands, palm open against palm, her thumbs centimetres away from her lips.

Bruna decided to kneel and was surprised that though she tried to keep Maria the focus of her invocations, it was Mario who kept appearing before her. When she brushed him aside, he was replaced by Sauro, Artemio's brother. She tried to concentrate harder and felt with satisfaction the increasing pain and numbness in her knees from the stone flagging. It was as though if she suffered, her prayers might be heard even louder.

On the fifth night of Maria's fever the rain came down in a wall so thick that the dogs wailed. Its hammering on the roof pulled Bruna out of bed to put containers under the spots where the shingles leaked. By morning the pots and pails were brimming, but the rain had stopped. Not for long, though – black clouds hovered overhead.

Bruna had used the early hours to boil barley. She strained it and held her daughter's head while Maria sipped gingerly, still not hungry. Bruna was relieved to see, though, that the child had strengthened a little. Her fever no longer raged, although it persisted, like smouldering ashes that would not be extinguished. Bruna was immensely cheered that she had not heard any of the noises or strange goings-on in the house that Signora Mazzetti had described. Her daughter did not appear hexed, nor had she developed any symptoms of disease. Therefore, it did indeed seem likely that Signora Mazzetti's initial diagnosis was correct: Maria had the frights, *le paure*.

While Maria's barley was boiling, Bruna had attended to her mushrooms. Squat, fat, with a verdant tinge, their juicy heads had already been braised and dried, so they were ready for storage. She sliced the *porcini* heads lengthways and packed them in layers of salt in a wooden box. Once she had dealt with her chickens, Ottavia's job after lunch would be to string the stalks together and hang them like prehistoric bone necklaces inside the fireplace to continue drying.

Artemio ate his breakfast while mulling over whether to dress the celery or sharpen his knives. He decided, while the rain held off, to cover and tie the celery in teepees of straw, to keep it white and tender during the early-morning frosts. When the clouds opened, he would work inside the house or the barn.

Mario came bouncing down the stairs as if the day had been declared work-free because of the inclement weather. He had finished fertilising the vegetable garden and orchard, but Artemio instructed him to go to the field to spread the manure and to mush the clods while he was at it. When Mario replied that the grain field would be drenched and a muddy bog, Artemio held his hand up to silence him. The quagmire work was punishment and he would brook no challenge. Enunciating every word clearly and slowly, he told Mario that he would feed the land its nutrients till Giubbotto made an appearance. Mario hunched angrily over his breakfast but did not argue.

Of their manager there'd been no sign. Every time the dogs barked, the family looked at each other alarmed. They expected Giubbotto to march into Poggio, the *carabinieri* by his side, and arrest Mario, or bribe them for Maria's hand, at any time. There was a constant feeling of nervous expectation. No one could predict the outcome, but whatever happened, the consequences of Mario's behaviour would affect everyone.

When the children had finished their bread and the first moist, fat, creamy walnuts of the season, Silvio was sent to the walnut trees to gather as many nuts from the ground and the branches as he could, before they were ruined by the rain. Looking like a street urchin from the city slums, he bolted out the door with no shoes on, only to be dragged back in again and told to put his clogs on. 'One child with a fever is quite enough, thank you,' scolded Bruna. Anna left to get the pigs out of their pen and run them for the day, and Fiamma did likewise with the sheep.

With the bustle of breakfast over and the children directed into their work, Bruna rinsed the breakfast dishes with the rainwater and sang a morning song about a woman whose goose escapes into her owners' beautiful living room and creates havoc. Before long, the song was interrupted by Ottavia's cries from the hen-run.

'Mamma! *Vieni!* Come! One of the brown hens has gone all floppy.'

Even before she'd picked up baby Pasquale and was out through the cheese room's back door, Bruna was thinking about chicken for dinner. Outside in the mud, she found one of her hen's high-stepping fernickety pecking had turned into a lopsided swoon. It was clearly suffering from old age. Losing no time, she put the baby down, popped the chicken under her arm, took its head in her other hand and wrung it out like a dripping sheet.

As she tied its scaly legs onto a hook in the corner of the yard to settle its blood at its neck, she smiled to herself, as pleased as a fox. Bruna called up to Ottavia to fetch the axe from the wood stack. What a wonderful soup for Maria!

Some time later, when Bruna was running her hands over her fowl's clammy skin, pondering how best to make the most of it, Artemio came back into the kitchen. Already plucked and washed, the chicken's head, neck, legs and claws had been chopped and placed in a large pot of water with the herb *salvastrella*, onion, celery, carrots, several potatoes and salt, and the soup's rich aroma was starting to fill the house with steamy promise.

On the table before her were the carcass and intestines, the latter coiled neatly on a wooden board, having been washed well with vinegar and salt. Bruna had decided to slice the intestines finely and was thinking that in a minute she would stoke the fire's flames high, and fry them with *porcini*, celery, parsley and onion (though perhaps, she thought, slipping her fingers absently through the slimy entrails, she would add some tomato *conserva* too) to have for lunch after the soup.

'I'll think I'll check on the chestnuts while the rain's holding off,' Artemio said, taking his chair from the fire to the table. Bruna nodded absently. Artemio frowned as he caught sight of the mixture that she was preparing. He leant in more closely, his expression suspicious. Once he had ascertained that the mushy slivers before him were in fact intestines, not worms, he sat back and relaxed.

Bruna's thoughts had moved on to tomorrow's meal plan. She would fry the chicken's heart, kidneys and the rest of its gizzards with onion before pouring two eggs over the top to make a *cibreo,* which means 'food fit for a king'. The white meat from the bird she would also prepare tomorrow, boiled to make another broth for Maria, perhaps with beans. They would eat that for tomorrow's dinner. By sundown the next day, not a trace of the chicken would remain, every morsel of meat (including the skin) eaten, its stripped bones devoured by the dogs. Even its feathers were put aside in a drawstring pouch along with goose feathers, to be sold to the quilt man when he next passed through.

'Pack me some food and I'll eat it up there.'

Bruna switched her attention to Artemio and stepped away from her chicken, rinsing her hands from the double-spouted copper jug of water that always sat on the kitchen sink.

'You'll not come home for lunch? There are chicken feet!' It was Artemio's favourite. She gathered bread and pecorino cheese and wrapped them up in a cloth.

'No, I'd like to spend some time with my trees, see when they're likely to be ready. I have to pick those gatherers up in two weeks. The boys will sleep in the barn and the Emilia Romagna girls will take their bed,' he answered, then took his lunch and left for the woods.

On the sixth day after Mario bashed Giubbotto, Maria's fever broke. She laid her amulet down and declared she wanted to help sort the dried rosemary and sage. 'Are the figs dry now?' she wanted to know, sitting up in bed. Could she pack them away in the larder for her mother?

Bruna was elated. She removed the fig leaf from under Maria's bed and ceremoniously placed it in a glass of water on the mantlepiece. On the same day, the clouds retreated, taking with them their oppressive gloom. And, as if he knew that there was good reason to raise a glass, Il Mangiatore came by to drop off the family's freshly milled corn.

'I have news for the Brunis,' he roared at the door. 'Where is Mario? I must tell him of Giubbotto.'

Mario was summoned from the roof, where he was laying stones on the loose slates that were letting the rain through.

'Quickly!' called Bruna and Artemio, both of them anxious to hear the news.

When the whole family was assembled, Il Mangiatore began importantly, 'Giubbotto, the manager that we all share, has not gone to the police!'

None of the Brunis cheered, as Il Mangiatore had expected they would.

'Don't you understand? Giubbotto is ignoring the incident!'

Artemio and Bruna looked at each other, traces of fear in their faces. If Mario was in the clear, then Maria was still in trouble.

'But he must be doing something,' said Bruna, confused.

'He is slandering your son, woman. Giubbotto is doing his best to black-ban Mario from ever harvesting again. He is spreading the word throughout Casentino that Mario is unhinged, deranged. According to Giubbotto, Mario's murderous temper will kill someone one day and he should be shunned at all costs.' Il Mangiatore searched out the Brunis' faces, while his own broadened into a smile.

'Giubbotto says he will not pursue Mario before the criminal justice courts because that would not be fair to the Bruni family. It is, after all, not your fault that your son is mad. He says you should not be made to suffer with the removal of the only other grown man to work your land.'

'Did he say anything of Maria during these rants?' asked Bruna.

'No. It is thought that because he wants nothing to do with Mario, he naturally wants nothing at all to do with Maria.' Il Mangiatore let out a triumphant belly laugh. He walked towards Mario and gave him a loud slap on the back. 'Come on! Mario should be congratulated.'

'Is that really the end of it?' Bruna was unwilling to believe their difficulties were over so easily.

Il Mangiatore raised his arms in the air. 'Yes!' he cried.

Artemio knew then that Giubbotto was scared witless of Mario. Poggio's manager would take no action because he feared for his life. He had taken Mario at his word that if he tried to marry his sister, Mario would kill him. None of it gave Artemio any pride or pleasure. His family's name was being bandied about and sullied. They had lost their honour and respectability. What's more, Giubbotto's story of sympathy for the Bruni family was so false as to be laughable. Still, he felt relief. Maria could start to live her life again, without a constant threat hanging over her head. Artemio thought that, in the end, if Giubbotto had ever come to him and threatened to take him to the forest guards for stealing a tree unless he gave him Maria's hand, he would gladly have taken a fine or been removed from his farm. He could never have seen his daughter married into a life of sadness with a man like Giubbotto. Perhaps now they could focus on their move to Campo Alto. The sooner they left Poggio, the better.

Il Mangiatore was shaking Mario's hand. Mario returned the pressure with a sardonic grin.

'Your sister is fortunate to have a brother who cares for her so much. You have saved her from a terrible fate.'

Looking fragile from her fever, Maria coughed and said nothing. Her mother noticed that heat had risen to her cheeks and that she had an air of sadness, as soft as a sheer veil. It made her appear more vulnerable than ever.

Il Mangiatore went on to say that he was confident Giubbotto would not bother them again. Apparently, he had sworn that he would not return to Poggio till the Brunis had relocated to their new farm.

Bruna listened to it all, her face apprehensive, her nervousness betrayed by a tightness about her mouth. She was not so confident. Surely Giubbotto would not let the matter drop so easily. A shudder of disgust passed through her. He was a vindictive man. He had been humiliated in front of his employees and was biding his time, that was all. It was simply not possible that Giubbotto would allow Mario's attack to go unavenged.

9

October

They slashed through the trees with great cracks and thuds, shredding leaves into ribbons along their way, hitting the ground aggressively. It was as though the woods were under attack.

The chestnuts were ready.

Artemio, a good two kilometres from his woods, stood thinking, worry creasing his brow. When the first ones fell, the big guns that were loaded with the casings of four or five chestnuts, he heard them clearly. The smaller ones would follow and begin to slam into the ground too. On their way, they would take out the double nut casings, so that the ricocheting built up to a crescendo, like corn exploding in a pan.

It was dangerous to visit them now. His trees were like angry giants pitching pin-covered cannonballs. He had to leave them in peace and let them bear their fruit on their own.

The continuous sound of ripping wood, dull impacts on earth, then scuttles and rustles, carried on with increasing ferocity over the next two weeks, till chestnuts carpeted the ground, in some places knee deep. As though spent, their casings were no longer brilliant green, but a muted pea-brown.

When more than eight days had passed, Artemio went to see his trees. He could smell the forest floor. It exuded a rich aroma of dew mingled with life and decay.

Artemio bent to examine his chestnut harvest. The spiky coverings had split to reveal swollen, brown nuts. To Artemio they were beautiful, the perfect homage to fertility.

On the second Tuesday of October, Artemio stepped outside the house into a dense mist that spread across the landscape like a wispy ghost with inquisitive fingers. As he walked towards the barn, he could hear Bruna trilling a new morning song, louder and happier than usual. He gave a rare smile, if only to himself. He knew that Bruna's excellent spirits were due to the female company he would bring home with him from the markets. Together with the *sensale*, the gatherers from Emilia Romagna would be waiting for him in Stia this morning. Artemio started to whistle at the thought. Those women were a sign of the success to come. A marvellous harvest with employees to collect it! His dreams were finally becoming a reality.

When Artemio entered the barn and shut the door behind him, Bruna's ballad was drowned out by the April lambs. At six months old they were separated from their mothers overnight and when approached they bellowed like full-throated men.

Careful not to disturb the hat that he had placed at a rakish angle on his head, Artemio threw a sack of walnuts over his shoulder. He was hoping to sell the nuts at the markets and buy the Mazzettis a few boiled barley sweets with part of the proceeds. They had done so much to help pull Maria through her illness that he wanted to buy them something extra special.

Back outside again, he shoved one hand deep into his pocket for warmth and immediately regretted not stuffing his wood-soled shoes with newspaper. The cold from the earth was already eating into his feet, travelling up his legs and into his bones. When he had gone some hundred metres down the mountain, the fog thickened into a cloud and he could see only three steps ahead, no more. The air smelt like river dirt and as he breathed it felt as though globules of water were clinging to the insides of his nostrils.

A small distance further, behind the curtain of cloud, he heard a woman calling to a bleating goat. She sounded panicky. The goat had undoubtedly chewed through its rope and wandered onto the public land patrolled by the zealous forest guards. No grazing without permission. That was the law, and as surely as a chestnut prick would poison your finger, fines would follow. Or perhaps it had strayed onto private land. Blinded as he was by the mist, he could not really tell where he was. If the goat was on private land, the woman's luck was no better. Someone would get her for compensation for that greedy old goat.

The woman sensed Artemio's movement in the mist and her calls to the goat became more frantic.

'*Tranquilla, Signora! Sono Bruni, del Poggio!* Don't worry, Signora! I am Bruni, of Poggio!'

'Thanks be to our merciful Mary, Mother of God!' the woman called back with relief. 'And bless you, sir, for identifying yourself. My husband left with the others and I'm forever chasing this fox. I can't even see the poxy beast today, let alone grab it.'

'Shepherd or shearer?' Artemio called into the fog.

'A shepherd, sir.'

'Good luck to you, Signora, and may God speed your husband's return.'

Artemio thought of the woman, alone now except for her elderly and young. Her husband had gone with the five thousand other men of Casentino in the annual exodus called the *transumanza* – people on the move. Unable to feed their livestock in the coming snow, they were taking them to the warmer lowlands.

Artemio passed a Madonna shrine on the roadside and crossed himself in thanks that he, too, did not have to pack up his sheep and herd them, along with the thousands of other flocks, to Maremma, on the southern coast of Tuscany. Artemio preferred staying home. It kept him to his purpose. He did not mind keeping his livestock locked up in his barn during the colder months, heating their water daily over the fire and feeding them grain grown especially for the winter months. It meant he was around to keep an eye on his chestnuts. But he had only fifteen sheep, while the real sheep tenders ran huge flocks and they depended solely on the production of their cheese. They had no choice but to walk the two-hundred-kilometre route through Chianti, to arrive at the malaria-ridden swamps of Maremma only to turn around and come back home again in March.

The forced migration was a great shame, Artemio thought. The men's departure left Casentino in disarray. When they were home, their hundreds of thousands of hectares of beautiful woodlands were as regal as a Medici garden. The men weeded, trimmed and cultivated the groves to perfection, not an acre was overlooked. But when they left, no one took care of the trees. The women did what they could, but with the orchards and vegetables and goats and oxen, they had no time or muscle for forest care. Artemio considered himself fortunate: he had a choice.

A few years earlier, though, his fortune had not been so good and he'd had no alternative but to send Silvio off with the *transumanza*. A streamer cloud had moved towards Poggio from the south. It had hovered over Bibbiena, its bottom flat and grey, its top a high black anvil. It had brought hail the likes of which few could remember. He'd stood at his front door and watched as his year's work was destroyed in ten minutes, listening to the hail as it hissed down like a steam train. When he went out to examine his losses, he'd had to shuffle his feet so as not to lose his footing. Like tiny bullets the hailstones had pelted his grain, apples, pears, plums and tomatoes, piercing everything with holes the size of a man's thumbnail. His cabbage heads were in tatters, the cherry and fig trees stripped. They'd survived the cold months on chestnuts, walnuts and whatever pecorino his sheep had provided that summer. That was the winter he'd hired his daughters out as maids. Anna had been eleven and Fiamma nine. Silvio, at seven years old, was packed off with the shepherds. Artemio would never forget it. The boy was paid *one* shoe for his wages. Half a year's work and a two-hundred-kilometre walk to be given just *one* shoe, not even two. Maybe they thought he'd come back the next year to earn the other shoe. Artemio would not send him again, though. He was still outraged at that injustice.

Adjusting the sack over his shoulder, Artemio thought back to his own childhood, when he, too, had been sent to another home. He'd been eight years old and had been delivered to a wealthy family just outside Florence, by a stranger driving a passing cart that his father had hailed. He had worked as a stable and field hand for four years, along with several other Casentino lads, all of them just as poor as he.

Sauro, Artemio's younger brother, had been kept at home, and when Artemio had given it deeper consideration, he'd understood that their friendship had begun to cool after his return.

Born in October 1867, Sauro was a winter baby, so he did not see the sun until April the next year. Following the Tuscan custom of swaddling, their mother had bound Sauro tightly and kept him warm and indoors throughout his first winter. By the summer of the following year he'd become sickly, constantly wailing, so she continued to keep him indoors, anxious about sudden chill winds. Sauro did not feel the sun bathe his skin till the summer of 1869, when he was almost two years old, and by then he suffered from such a lack of vitamin D, he had developed rickets. The condition was not so unusual for weak babies, but Sauro's bones became so soft he could not walk until he was five years old. When he did manage to hoist himself up, the bones in his legs were like cheese and they sank into curved sticks under the weight of his body. Artemio, with his own bandy legs and barrel chest, had probably suffered from the same illness, but it was never serious enough for anyone to notice. When Artemio observed the older men at Stia, many of them looked as though they had been born and raised on a horse. They had more than likely all suffered from a lack of sunshine, but they'd all grown up strong enough in the end.

Artemio remembered coming home from Florence at twelve years old and seeing how his brother was still being pampered by their mother. She hovered over him like a cat ready to clamp her jaws around her kitten's neck and carry it off to the safe warmth of the fireplace, indoors, still, even after she'd been advised to keep him outside and work him to strengthen his skeleton. Then their father began to prefer Artemio's company over Sauro's, searching him out for guidance on how best to forge a nail or fit a plank. Sauro saw his father and brother consult each other and grew jealous of the affection and respect they shared. His two older sisters watched the relationship thicken and mature, unfazed. It never occurred to them to be jealous, as they shared no interests or duties with the men. Deep voices hummed to a different tune of life. The girls were guided and chided by the shrill calls of their mother, whose undertaking it was to prepare them to be good wives.

Ultimately, Sauro grew into a lazy but pleasant adolescent accustomed to being treated like an invalid. When he passed his First Holy Communion and Artemio's father bemoaned the fact that they would have no meat for the celebration feast, the woodpeckers were Artemio's idea. He'd found them, high up in the birch tree down near the wood stack. There were at least seven. After watching them grow fat during spring, he shimmied up the tree to snatch them, just as they were about to fly from their mother's nest for the first time. His own mother hugged him for his ingenuity. She crowned the birds with sage and rosemary and roasted them in garlic oil. But when Sauro came home from church, with the sequined string around his forehead to show he'd taken his first communion, he refused to touch them. Their mother begged him to eat something, while the rest of the Bruni family marvelled at how fine the chicks tasted. But Sauro retorted, 'I'm not *that* hungry.' The woodpeckers still haunted Artemio, after all these years.

The impact of the *transumanza* could be seen in Stia's piazza. Two-and-a-half-thousand men had deserted the town and the many farms around it. Manning most of the produce stalls, which had reduced in size and number, were women, buried underneath headscarves and shawls. There were also the *barrocciai*. They were rough, ill-mannered men who travelled up and down the isolated roads on carts. They purchased coal from coal makers in the forests and brought it down to town to sell to the villagers. The *barrocciai* were known for drinking away their profits, before setting out on the roads again and running people down with their drunk driving.

Artemio strode towards a group of men he knew well, thinking to catch up on the town's news before negotiating the sale of his walnuts and collecting his workers. His friends greeted him with talk of the wolves again. It seemed that several families higher up towards Mount Falterona had lost lambs. Towards Campo Alto too, one friend warned him. A pack had come in the middle of the night and mauled two sheep for pleasure. They'd killed the dogs for good measure. The owners had heard the barks and bleats, but had not emerged in time to save their animals.

The talk moved on to wine, which was apparently fine, but early, with the grapes a good fifteen to twenty days ahead of schedule. Many wine makers were already well into their *vendemmia* (grape harvest). Some of Artemio's friends had also heard that Maria's persistent fever had passed and that she was now well. These men smiled at Artemio, to show they shared his relief at his daughter's good health.

Out of the corner of his eye, Artemio saw a woman and a girl crouching beside some chickens in a wooden crate. On top of the crate they'd placed a collection of eggs inside a nest of straw. From the girl's striking blonde hair, he guessed the couple were the new mother and daughter from Romena. A village boy walked slowly in front of them, pretending he was interested in their wares, his clothes as slick as his hair. His matronly mother, all broad breasts and feathered bonnet, walked behind him. She noticed her smart young son staring at the pretty farm girl. With a sharp finger she nudged him along, as one would a pedigree dog intent on sniffing out a mongrel. Artemio folded his arms across his chest and looked beyond them.

Not twenty metres away, descending the piazza with two women and Il Rosso, was the *sensale*. It was Il Rosso who made them hard to miss amid the crowd. His hair glowed like a red lantern in the grey morning light.

Artemio picked up his sack and left his friends to join the *sensale*.

'*Buon giorno*, Signor Sensale,' Artemio said genially, before nodding curtly at Il Rosso and turning to the women to greet them too.

'*Buon giorno*, Bruni,' the *sensale* responded cheerfully. 'It's a good autumn for wine and chestnuts. You have fared as well as you foresaw?'

'I have, Signor Sensale. And you have my women, I see,' Artemio replied.

'Your *woman*!' corrected Il Rosso, cutting in quickly.

Artemio glanced at the *sensale*, who was looking quizzically at Il Rosso.

'No, my *women*. I requested *two* women to be brought over from Emilia Romagna.'

Il Rosso splatted his open palm against his forehead and raised his eyes towards heaven. Loudly, so that all within hearing distance could hear, he guffawed. 'Big Littlelegs is having momentary memory loss, not so uncommon for *mezzadro* farmers, I'm told. You ordered one woman and so did I. That means one of these charming ladies will help you collect your chestnuts, the other will help me.' At the sound of Il Rosso's argumentative voice, passers-by turned to stare, along with Artemio's group of friends.

'What?' Artemio looked at Il Rosso, bewildered. It was as though the redhead were speaking in a language he could not understand. He'd had this feeling before, on Sundays at mass when the priest recited the service in Latin. The Catholic Church did not deliver sermons in Italian so the faithful could understand. Sacraments and prayers were repeated over and over again in Latin. Artemio often found himself frustrated, trying to watch how the priest moved his lips so he could sound out the words. But the clergyman kept his back to the people, only permitted to observe worship facing the altar. Artemio looked at Il Rosso dumbly.

'*One* for you and *one* for me,' Il Rosso said, saying his words clearly as though speaking to a deaf man.

Artemio turned to face the *sensale*. 'What is he saying, Signor Sensale?'

'Well, clearly there is some discrepancy with this contract,' the *sensale* stammered. 'Claudio, are you sure that you and Bruni split the order for these women? Was it not that he ordered two and you were the witness to that request?'

At the *sensale*'s questions, Il Rosso snapped. 'By God, man! Are you implying that I am a liar?' Il Rosso's face was scarlet with rage. His flaccid lips had spittle in their corners and he spat white flecks of sticky saliva as he shouted. Artemio was astounded that the man had become so angry so quickly.

'No, no, no.' The *sensale* held up both hands for calm. 'This contract is under question, obviously. That is all I can say. Bruni says he booked two women but you say you both booked one each. Claudio, you are our witness. Legally we are bound by you.' The *sensale* appeared just as confused as Artemio.

Turning to address the crowd that had gathered, Il Rosso yelled, 'You all saw me, no? Acting as a witness to Artemio Bruni's deal? In the same deal I myself brought a woman over too. Is that so unusual?'

Artemio became aware of the people watching, their eyes glued to what was fast becoming an unpleasant spectacle. He saw Giovanni, from the village of Consuma, who had been at his wedding to Bruna because their fathers had cut wood together. He was standing with Marcello the baker, who had lost an eye when a chestnut exploded in a pan near his face. Beside him was Elio, whom Artemio liked enormously as he spoke little and because years ago he'd lent Artemio a piece of tarpaulin to keep him dry on the way home. These were the same men that moments earlier had given him *tanti saluti* (their best regards) to pass on to Bruna for the health of their daughter. They stood silently, watching the scene play out before them. Artemio realised that not one of them would come forward to support his claim. They had to look after their own futures, their own deals, which could be ruined if they came to his defence. If Il Rosso, or a friend of his, were ever called to witness one of their agricultural pursuits, Il Rosso would never forget their public protection of Artemio.

Still, every man observing this transaction knew that Il Rosso's performance was a sham. The *sensale* clearly owed Il Rosso a favour. Everyone already knew that the estimator would not uphold Artemio's agreement because Il Rosso was calling his favour in. Loans, aid, vendettas, promotions, they were currency to be cashed in or traded against when the moment presented itself. Il Rosso's bluster was too rehearsed to ring true, but the *sensale* would have to accommodate the land owner, not the land renter.

With his back erect, Artemio took two steps towards Il Rosso so that he was inches away from the man's face.

'*I* call you a liar! And you will go to purgatory for your deceit. Recant and return your family's honour!' Artemio shoved his face closer still and his voice grew soft, till it was a whisper. 'You lazy bastard. You never checked your trees. You simply realised too late that you had more chestnuts than you could handle, so you decided to take what is rightly mine.'

Il Rosso stepped away from Artemio, wheezing with anger. He pointed his finger at him. '*My* family's honour? Take the log out of your own eye before you point out the splinter in mine! You will regret those words, Bruni. For I am no liar and the law is on my side.'

Quiet till now, the *sensale* put his hand on Artemio's upper arm and gripped hard, in case Artemio decided to lunge at Il Rosso. Artemio was breathing deeply and loudly through his nose. 'Bruni,' the *sensale* said quickly, 'my apologies. But I must stand by my witness's word. When you take on Campo Alto, we will meet again.' Artemio had no idea what the man was talking about, but he knew he had to surrender.

Facing off Il Rosso, his chest throbbing with anger and frustration, Artemio caught sight of the two women. They were backing away, understandably frightened by the conflict. They were mother and daughter. Thin, tired-looking women with angular faces and bony noses. He could not afford to lose a gatherer now and they could still turn around and go home.

'Come,' he said to the older of the two, the mother, 'we will prepare for tomorrow's harvest.'

Il Rosso looked at him victoriously. He put his hand on the daughter's shoulder.

The people made way for Artemio and his worker as they walked through the crowd. He walked proudly, the woman slightly behind him, with her head down. Before Artemio was too far away, as the crowd fell into his wake, Il Rosso called out to him and made him turn.

'You know, I have red hair for a reason. If you rub me the wrong way I will catch fire. Like a match, I will explode. Watch it, Gambine, you will see my flames.'

This was the fight, over the women from Emilia Romagna, that even one hundred years later would not be forgotten. And those were the words, when Il Rosso likened himself to a match, that would be passed from farmer to son for decades to come. For three generations the Bruni family carried a grudge against Il Rosso and his clan. So when the end finally came for Artemio, the Brunis and the people of Stia had no doubt where to point the finger.

10

Chestnut harvest day dawned with all the brilliance that a Casentino family could hope for from their most special day. Deep blue skies spread out above the auburn trees, turning the mountains into a tapestry of red, bronze, amber and green, with the crystal air giving each leaf a sharp clarity.

The Brunis and their worker had left Poggio at four in the morning, when the stars in the pool of ink above them sparkled with wintry brightness. By their sides they swung wooden buckets, sacks, chestnut twig brooms and forked branches. On their feet they wore shoes with hardy nails hammered into their soles, so that no one would slip into a bed of razor-sharp needles. To protect their heads against the spiky nuts that plummeted from great heights, they wore make-do helmets of wax paper under doubled-over scarves.

Today the family planned to work straight through till sunset; there would be no break for lunch. They had to harvest swiftly and stockpile chestnuts before the wild boars, rot, rain and damp claimed them. Only Bruna would slip away early to feed the animals and prepare dinner. She would leave with baby Pasquale, whom Ottavia was to watch all day at a safe distance from the chestnuts.

From the hillsides around them they could hear dozens of families rustling about on their own slices of woodland. Mules brayed; a child called 'Teh, teh, drrrrr' to her sheep; and deep, animated voices yelled commands. The day was so clear that neighbours could be identified and every word understood.

'Hold on to the ladder for me.' 'Here! Here! Bring me a sack!' 'Oh! Lovely! Look at this great heap!' By mid-morning one family had started to sing.

Oh, beautiful is our chestnut, in its elegant clothes.
It's a fruit of the mountains, sweet and tasty those.

Four more verses outlining the virtues of the chestnut followed, and soon every plunge and plateau resounded with the well-known song. The Brunis' Emilia Romagna woman stumbled across the lyrics, trying to learn the Tuscan words and intonations. She gave up in the end, laughing and brandishing her broom at everyone.

Work progressed more quietly once imaginary lines had been determined between the signal trees that marked the borders of the Bruni land. The family was then free to sweep up their boundaries, to avoid ownership confusion. The tracks and pathways were cleared so no chestnuts would be crushed by the oxen and *treggia* during transportation back to the *seccatoio*. Then everyone broke out to gather alone, the children just as focused as the adults.

And still the chestnuts continued to fall. On the ground they looked like tiny hedgehogs curled into themselves for protection. Most casings held three or four chestnuts. A rare find, which inspired shouts of victory or a 'Wheh-ah!', was one as big as a woman's fist, that held five or six. The rarest of all, though, were the 'virgins', the ones with only one chestnut. They were treated with a quiet esteem, as though they were somehow holy.

To sort through the spikes and poke the chestnuts out of their casings, most people used big forks or long tongs, *grappelle*, that were carved especially for the job. If the needles would not relinquish their nuts, the casings were gently prodded with a foot or poked out carefully with fingers, then put in a sack.

All day long, Bruna kept her head down as she gathered and swept. She preferred to use the basket with the sturdy wooden handle. It was made to lean on while bending and collecting uphill, so that the strain was kept off her back. When it was full, she carried it over to the main heap that would soon be carted back to the *seccatoio*. She smiled at the rising pile and thought that it was indeed a very fine year for chestnuts.

In her pause, her hand wandered to her petticoat's secret pocket. Artemio had not confided in her his hopes for this crop – no whispered words on their pillows late at night about his plans for the money it would bring them. Artemio always kept his thoughts to himself. He had not told her of the events at the Stia markets the previous day. He'd come home with only one woman and thrown the words 'Il Rosso took the other one' at her and left that poor woman standing in the kitchen looking like a rabbit stuck in the corner of a cage.

Bruna had soon started her talking about her children, though. To get a woman to relax, one must ask about her babies. Once the woman's concerns about her daughter, to whom she had not even said goodbye, were eased with the slightly comforting words that Il Rosso was not an evil man, just a greedy one, she relaxed. Her appetite was not sufficiently curtailed by her worry to stop her eating nine slices of grilled polenta with rosemary salt and olive oil, either. Bruna had suspected that the women would arrive starving after their walk over the Alps, and Our Sainted Mary knew there wasn't much food in the high parts of Emilia Romagna! The Romagna side of the mountains was even steeper than Casentino. If one stood at the top of Mount Falterona and looked down to Tuscany, it was green and lush. On the other side, just as if it had slipped God's mind, was Romagna, grey with rocks and brown with thistle. Impossible to coax much out of that rubble. Poorer than us, she sighed, but they always seemed happy enough.

When the two of them had made the woman's bed together, the woman had smoothed the sheets and recounted the Stia fight to her in detail. Bruna had not needed to prod and she was fortunate that the woman was not too hard to understand. The Romagna women she'd met in the past had chit-chatted away in gibberish, using different words with odd inflections, which no one except their own kind understood, even though their homes were only thirty kilometres away from Stia. So now she knew why Artemio had lain by her side last night like a lump of wet wood, before dragging the bedcovers over himself as if he were an undertaker spreading a shroud. He'd been cheated by the men above him.

With their double-dealing they'd defeated him at a time at which he had felt that what he wanted was within his reach. The snatching away of his worker was not a big problem in itself. They would manage without the second gatherer. It was the constant scheming of those in positions of power. They had won again and Artemio had been alternatively angry and miserable all day. She felt so sorry for him. He had shown none of the joy that he should have reserved for this, his best harvest.

At the end of the first day of the chestnut harvest, when the light softened with signs of dusk, before she called Ottavia and baby Pasquale, Bruna searched out Artemio. She found him bending under one of his ancient beauties, its arms outstretched above him like a doting grandfather. Artemio was gently gathering chestnuts from around the roots of its trunk. Bruna noticed that its branches still had a lot of food to offer. Most men would climb those branches, take to them with a big stick and bash the last ones down. But Artemio did not hold with that, he would wait till the tree bestowed him with its chestnuts; he would never harm a giver.

The damp leaves absorbed her footfalls as she came up behind him. When she put her hand on his shoulder, he stood and turned to look down at her. Again she saw the disappointment in his eyes. She moved closer to him, so that the heat from their bodies melded. His scent aroused an elemental feeling of love and life from deep within her.

'We can do it,' she said simply, before bringing her hand up to rest on his cheek. 'Like we always do, you and I, with the children, by ourselves.'

Artemio bent his head towards her and Bruna moved her hand around to his head. She let her fingers caress the swirl of hair at his neck, while he rested his head on her shoulder.

They stayed like that for a few minutes, the harvest momentarily forgotten for the first time in months, till Artemio pulled back his head. She saw that some of the shadow in his eyes was gone. It was enough. Her loving touch had swept away a little of the bitterness of defeat.

※

That night everyone plunged their hands into boiling water to sterilise the pricks from the chestnut shells. The adults barely even braced themselves, while the younger ones, whose fingers were not so callused, howled with pain. Bruna pushed Silvio's hands down deeper into the pot, to loosen the almost invisible splinters that would have to be dug out. He swore under his breath and stamped his feet. Better to braise him now than cut off his fingers when they were green with infection.

Dinner was a feast of *zuppetta di patate*, a stewed mixture of cubed potatoes, finely chopped onions, rosemary, sage, oil, tomato *conserva*, salt and water. When the potatoes were cooked through and almost mash, Bruna served them on top of thick slices of toast that had been rubbed with fresh cloves of garlic. At the last minute she poured a thin stream of oil on top.

The conversation at the table revolved, as it often did, around what food was in the winter pantry. The fresh seasonal summer vegetables, such as tomatoes, carrots, celery, lettuce, green beans, wild herbs and grasses, were gone. Nor would there be any more meat, such as sausages, prosciutto, bacon or salami, till this year's December pig was slaughtered.

'But our Maria was in the vegetable garden before the chestnuts fell. She has done the winter planting,' Bruna explained. 'The white onions will be ready in March, so we'll come back from Campo Alto for those. The winter salads –

endive, chicory and the curly black spinach, plus a little bit of white celery – will keep us over Christmas.'

'*Sotto la neve, pane; sotto l'acqua, fame.* Under the snow, you'll find bread; under the rain, you'll find hunger,' responded the woman from Emilia Romagna, with a sage nod. Bruna uttered an understanding 'Eh, eh eh!' to show that they shared the same expression. During the crystallised months, when snow covered their vegetable patches, it was a miracle of nature the way the winter lettuces kept so beautifully. Igloos formed like protective caps to keep the vegetables inside under perfect refrigeration. But if the temperatures rose with rain and the snow melted, all the greens rotted.

'We have potatoes, two bunches of spinach and onions in the larder,' added Anna.

'There are beans too,' Bruna said with a 'don't worry' tone to her voice. 'Along with whatever pecorino we don't need to sell. There's the wheat, a little polenta, walnuts and apples. We'll have to be careful with it all, though. We have a move to think about.'

'That'd certainly see my family through,' the woman said enviously.

'There'll be boiled chestnuts tomorrow night,' Bruna said, to stop the woman from getting too excited.

'Nothing wrong with that, thank the blessed Mother. When are you moving?'

They looked to Artemio, who was slicing bread. 'I'll be seeing my brother and the *sensale* when the chestnuts are all in and over their fire.'

'Oh, it's your brother's farm that you're taking on, then?'

Artemio nodded, his eyes on the bread.

'I'll pray for him,' the woman said consolingly. 'My very own uncle had to take on my father's farm when Papa was gored through the stomach by our bull. We had the only bull in Romagna for a hundred kilometres. It was a great black thing with a ring through its nose. Horns as long as your Maria's hair here. A splendid sire, with a fine seed – a good money-earner. Hated my father, though, from all the thrashings to break its spirit. My poor father bled to death in the end, God rest his soul.'

'My brother is quite well, thank you. He needs only prayers to help him work harder.'

'Well, I quite understand idleness and I certainly will pray for him. You'll be moving according to the law then, by 31 January? Shame it couldn't be before, but I guess your brother has his reasons. Horrible time to move, January.'

'We'll wait till then,' Artemio said shortly and closed the conversation.

After apples and walnuts, Bruna rose from the table and the family began to clear up and retire. Wearily the children went outside to relieve themselves, followed one by one by the adults, while Bruna wrapped and breastfed baby Pasquale. They moved to the fire for one round of the rosary before everyone fell asleep in upright positions.

When she had settled the baby, Bruna went back downstairs. Alone in the kitchen, she scrubbed and hung before the fire the previous night's nappy wraps, thinking to reappraise the week's food. She considered Il Mangiatore's polenta for tomorrow night, with slices of pecorino on top. That was the best idea, Bruna assured herself, their noses would catch that. She'd pour it onto a wooden cutting board so that everyone could help themselves. She would follow or team it with boiled spinach, pan fried in oil and garlic. Then they would have the traditional boiled chestnuts, the ones that celebrated the first harvest and were sucked or chewed out of their skins.

Too exhausted to hum and still with much to do, Bruna poured a sack of the day's harvest into a bucket of water to sit for nine days. The water preserved the chestnuts for up to two months. She'd slit them and roast them over the fire in a couple of weeks. Another sack would come back for steeping tomorrow, but no more, or Giubbotto would accuse them of stealing more than their half. He'd come to the woods tomorrow, more than likely. Giubbotto may have promised never to set foot on Poggio while the Brunis lived there, but he was still obliged to do his job and assess the farm's chestnuts for division.

She put the potato peelings in a bucket by the door for the compost, along with a bucket of slops for the dogs. After she had swept the floor, she banked the fire. Stepping away, she backed into a chair and sank into it, covering her face with her hands. Sleep would have overwhelmed her then, but she refused to give in to it. She sat up and rubbed her eyes. While she was trying to gather the strength to go up to bed, her mind wandered to Sauro's vegetable garden up at Campo Alto. She wondered how it was being prepared for the winter. From the little time she'd spent with her sister-in-law at baptisms, weddings and funerals, she'd gleaned that the woman had a perfectly good green thumb. Bruna hoped so, because she'd be inheriting her garden, and her love of cultivating vegetables and tending to the soil's needs, or lack of it, would be revealed in how well it helped her own seeds to germinate.

She recalled a conversation she had once had with her sister-in-law about *assenzio*, a refreshing tonic good for sore stomachs and kidney infections. It was made from boiled mallow, and her sister-in-law had said she was trying to grow mallow but that it was tricky with the wind up there. She'd had a fondness for *mimmi*, Bruna remembered, the sweet biscuits that were cut and baked into the shape of boys and girls at Easter time. She was a pretty woman, with a rosebud mouth. Small in stature, she was feminine and fragile, the kind of woman you'd least expect to have four nuggety sons.

Bruna remembered the joke they had shared at the First Holy Communion of Sauro's youngest son. They'd laughed gaily at how Sauro was the real Gambine, with his funny little bowlegs. Ironic how Artemio had acquired that nickname and not Sauro, they'd said, giggling behind their hands at their men. She'd felt a thrill of excitement at their disloyalty. It had felt good, even more so because it was a moment of intimacy with someone she liked but whose company she had always been denied. Her name was Amabile, not an uncommon name in Tuscany. It meant 'loveable', and Bruna thought that her sister-in-law probably was, if only she had been able to get to know her better.

With a deep sigh, Bruna forced herself to stand. Gathering up the scarves and bonnets the children had left scattered about the kitchen, she hung them along the clothes hooks beside the door and went up to bed.

In late October, the harvest was over and the family's focus shifted to their drying house, where the chestnuts lay waiting for their fires. Artemio's *seccatoio* branches creaked under the weight of his massive yield, which certainly seemed far more plentiful than anyone else's. To celebrate the eve of the chestnut fires, the Mazzettis invited the Brunis to join them and their two guests at the Ospita for *veglia*. That day, Felice, the travelling haberdashery man, also came lumbering up the Bruni family track, looking for a bed. But as the woman from

Emilia Romagna had already put the boys out of the house and into the barn, he had to be redirected to Signora Mazzetti's. Felice was waved off with promises that they would see him that very night for *veglia*.

Upon arrival for the gathering, Bruna glanced around the Mazzettis' kitchen, noticing with concern that the house was damper than ever. Every stone seemed to breathe a stale odour of old rainwater. It did not matter how many juniper branches Signora Mazzetti threw on the fire to sweeten the air, they could not mask the smell of wet mortar and cold clay. The roof appeared badly in need of maintenance, too. Bruna would have to send Mario down with some slate and rocks. He would need to see to the gaps in the windows as well. Stuff them with hay or little rolls of newspaper. The house would be as cold as a castle, and the Mazzettis, frail as they were, would be like reeds in a whistling wind, unless Bruna took action.

Signor Mazzetti was at the fire with Felice and the Ospita's other two guests – obviously coal makers. The coalies had been given the positions of honour, right before the grate. Both men were in their late forties, with skin that looked like a half-scrubbed chimney wall. Craggy, weather-beaten, the residue of soot and charcoal would be forever etched into the wrinkles of their foreheads and the laugh lines around their eyes. Their hands, the creases in their fingers, their cuticles, along with the hairs on their forearms, were all stained black, in varying degrees of intensity.

They sat with their arms crossed over their chests and their legs stuck straight out before them. Though neither of them smiled, there was something about them that suggested a cheerful contentedness. After three months in the most isolated pockets of the Casentino peaks, with only each other and their enormous log fires to keep them company, they were returning from Stia after having sold their charcoal. This was the first time in twelve weeks that they'd sat in a chair, under a roof, in front of a warm blaze, and they had every intention of enjoying it.

Felice sat beside them with an air of quiet expectancy. He was ready for the coalies to start telling their stories. Signor Mazzetti was crouched inside the huge hearth, shuffling chestnuts about in a great wrought-iron griddle. All four men's faces reflected the orange glow of the flames.

When Signor Mazzetti rose to greet the Brunis, his knees clicked with a snap so loud that one of the coalies called out, 'Aw, mamma mia! Don't come apart now!'

Signora Mazzetti, at the kitchen table poring over Felice's hooks, eyelets and buttons, called to the coalie reproachfully. 'Watch out, young man, because before too long your own knees will crick so loud you'll sound like an accordion and people will sing along to you as you walk.'

Everybody laughed at her protectiveness of her husband.

'Come, my dear Bruna, what do you need here?' she said, turning her attention to her friend. 'Where's your woman?'

'She's gone to visit her daughter for the evening at Il Rosso's,' replied Bruna, taking a place at the end of the table. She arranged her sack of walnuts on the floor beside her and her tray of dried figs in front of her. She wanted to make *picce* while listening to the evening's chatter. She would shell the walnuts, slice the figs, and then stuff a walnut into each one, along with a little aniseed. Tomorrow she'd tie them securely into paper bags with plenty of bay leaves to keep out the weevils. The *picce* would not be seen again till Christmas Day, when she'd put them on the table after lunch for sweets.

'You too, girls, come on. Settle in before you touch the chestnuts,' Signora Mazzetti called.

Maria, Anna and Fiamma came over to the table with their extra lamps and trousseaus. They were working on their embroidery, pillowcases being the fashion of the moment, though by the time they married, each girl hoped to have sheets, towels and at least one tablecloth. Maria was aiming at a veil, and perhaps a baptism wrap for her first baby, too. A girl who had all these things was a rich bride, as their stitches were like cash in the bank. Their trousseaus could be sold for good money should they need it. If any of the girls married and died without an heir, it would be returned to Bruna and Artemio, who could sell, keep or pass it on to the grandchild of their choice.

'What did I want to say?' puzzled Signora Mazzetti, her finger on her chin. The girls looked at the old woman patiently while Signor Mazzetti threw another log on the fire. The cinders exploded like fireflies with his toss.

'Oh yes, Mario decided to stay with his tools in the barn, eh? What's he hiding in there? Funny boy. Don't know how he can stand the smell of all that animal piss. It's like acid.'

'He's probably down at Podervecchio. It doesn't matter. The boy has to have some fun.'

'Hmm,' said Signora Mazzetti thoughtfully.

As the women fell silent, Signor Mazzetti steadied his griddle on the iron tripod over the flames and went over to sit next to Artemio, who had pulled up a chair beside the coalies. Artemio ignored baby Pasquale, who was tugging insistently on his trouser leg, trying to pull himself up. Signor Mazzetti reached over and gave the baby his finger. With a throaty chortle, baby Pasquale grasped it tightly and waddled slowly towards Signor Mazzetti, till he was wedged happily between the elderly man's knees. One of the coalies then turned to Felice and started to tell a joke.

'There was this farm manager who got a beautiful young farm girl pregnant. So the farm manager asked the farmer for his daughter's hand. They married, and four and a half months later, the girl had a baby. Suspecting some hanky-panky before the wedding night, the girl's father, the farmer, goes to his manager and says, "If it takes nine months to have a baby, how come it took my daughter only four and a half months?" The farm manager replied, "Because four and a half days plus four and a half nights make nine months. What's your problem?" And the farmer *believed* the manager!'

Felice was the only one who laughed. Artemio's back stiffened slightly. Bruna put her hands inside her sack and ran her fingers through the walnuts, rattling the shells together, irritated. She wondered what Maria had made of the coalie's joke with its dumb farmer and beautiful daughter. Its significance would not be lost on her, even though she was now feigning a deep concentration on her needlework. God forbid that the child's life would always be haunted by the advances of arrogant men above her. The joke perfectly expressed how stupid they thought farmers were. Exasperated, she rattled the walnuts more insistently.

Would the coalie tell the story of the manager at Pelago who got a pretty girl pregnant before throwing the whole family off their farm? It had happened a couple of years before in November, just as the snows were coming. The girl had been quite large when the manager dismissed them. Eight people suffered at the hands of that cruel man. They were destitute till the wealthy Frescobaldi wine family at Pomino was told of their plight and offered the family one of their *seccatoios*. The family moved in, slept on the dirt floor and cooked over an outdoor fire throughout the frigid winter. The girl delivered her baby in the *seccatoio*. Would the coalies laugh at that? The Frescobaldis eventually saw what a good, honest family they were and gave them a small farm and house to look after. Bruna clacked her walnuts more loudly still, until Maria looked up.

'Mamma, please. It's all right,' she said in a whisper.

Bruna stopped her rattling and tutted instead.

'How is your husband's tooth?' asked Anna. Signora Mazzetti, who had not heard the joke, looked up from Felice's button selection.

'Bad, thank you for asking. Blessed man will not let me touch him. Moans in his sleep.' The candle on the table guttered, prompting Signora Mazzetti to rise and fetch a fresh one.

Before long, Signor Mazzetti announced the chestnuts were ready and the girls put aside their embroidery. He tipped the swollen and charred chestnuts out of the pan and into a square of material. Wrapping them tightly, he put the bundle on the table and leant his body weight onto them, so that their skins cracked apart under the heels of his hands. Opening the cloth, he scattered the hot nuts across the table. The sound made the coalies turn their heads, and Signor Mazzetti waved them over. Soon everyone was crammed along the wooden benches at the table and every fingertip was black with charcoal from the burnt skins. The air filled with crunches, snaps and the sweet smell of chestnut steam.

'Uffa!' groaned Signor Mazzetti after his body had spasmed with pain.

'What's the matter?' asked one of the coalies, looking concerned.

'This putrid tooth,' he cried, cradling his jaw, close to tears. 'I can't stand it any more.'

'Let me see,' said the man as he reached his big hand slowly towards Signor Mazzetti's mouth. 'My father ... was ...

good,' he muttered under his breath while he eased Signor Mazzetti's bottom lip down with his thumb, '... with ... rotten ...' As quick as a bird's peck he grabbed Signor Mazzetti's long, yellow tooth and yanked it clean out. '... TEETH!' he yelled jubilantly.

There was a stunned silence around the table. Nobody moved. They stared at the coalie as he waved the tooth about, as if it were a trophy. Signor Mazzetti, whose mouth began to pour blood like an overturned wine flask, went pale.

'It's out! It's out!' shrieked Signora Mazzetti, jumping up to run around the table. A chorus of giggles, roars of laughter and yells followed. Blood, tears and saliva ran down Signor Mazzetti's shocked face, but slowly he began to smile, just before his wife mercifully rested a clean tea towel on his chin for him.

'Clamp down on it, man!' cried the coalie. 'The bleeding will stop soon. Courage; it's all over. My father was a blacksmith with a fondness for pulling teeth. The element of surprise. It's the only way!'

'Saints alive, I was going to take you out tonight and tie that tooth up to a lowered branch, before letting the branch go,' chuckled Artemio.

Signora Mazzetti helped her husband up and drew him over to the fire. She fussed inside her cupboards for herbs to help stem the bleeding while the others continued to sit around the table, eating their chestnuts, celebrating the long-awaited extraction of Dentino's (Littletooth's) famous canine.

When the excitement had died down, baby Pasquale started to grizzle and rub his fists against his eyes. It was time, Bruna decided, to sneak off to the stool in the back corner of the hearth and drape a shawl from her neck to her knees, so as to give him his bedtime breastfeed. When he'd had his fill, she rocked him, holding his smooth cheek to hers, patting his back. Lost in his warm scent, she started to sing a lullaby. Little by little, the group around the table grew silent and listened to her. After a few lines, Felice joined in with Bruna, his tone rich and emotional. Then the Mazzettis added their voices, thin and quivery. The coalies combined their basses, pitching low, till finally her own children began to sing the lullaby too. In the dark room, candlelight illuminated the faces of the men and women. Their eyes mirrored memories of this *ninna nanna*, and the mothers and grandmothers who had sung it to them.

Ninna-nanna, nanna oh!
Il bambino a chi lo do?
Se lo do alla Befana,
Me lo tiene una settimana;
Se lo do all' uomo nero,
Me lo tiene un anno intero.
Ninna-nanna, nanna, fate,
Il bambino addormentate!
S'addormenti nella culla,
Con Gesu e la Madonna!

Ninna-nanna, nanna oh!
Who will I give this baby to?
If I give him to the good witch,
She'll keep him for a week;
If I give him to the black man,
He'll keep him for a whole year.
Ninna-nanna, nanna, do as I say,
Go to sleep, little baby!
If you sleep in your bassinette,
You'll be with Jesus and Mary.

On the way home that night, the coalie's joke forgotten, a peace that Bruna had not felt in a long time began to settle in her heart. She held her husband's arm tightly; the night that enveloped them was so dark, there was no beginning, middle or end to the space around them. The children walked ahead of their parents, giddy in the infinite blackness. To stay grounded, they shone their lanterns onto their feet.

'You've plenty of milk, haven't you?' inquired Artemio suddenly.

For a second, Bruna had no idea what he was talking about. She could not recall him having ever asked about her supply of breastmilk. It was a given between them that her flow was ample.

'Yes, there is no problem.'

'Good. I've decided that we will foster an orphan. *Gli Innocenti* [The Innocents – the Orphanage of the Abandoned] pay a good monthly fee for mother's milk. We need the money.'

Bruna said nothing as she tried to absorb this news.

'As soon as we shift everything up to Campo Alto, I'll go to Florence and pick up a baby.'

Bruna looked down at Pasquale, wrapped securely in his blanket, deep in slumber.

'Don't you think we should discuss this further? The child will need clothes, food, attention and love.'

'My parents will care for it. All you have to do is feed it,' responded Artemio curtly.

Had he no idea what it took to raise a child? Didn't he see her chores? What would it take for him to notice the fatigue that made her cry when no one was looking? Bruna loosened her grip on his arm, feeling an inexplicable sense of loss. It was as though Artemio had stolen something from her. In his determination to own land, he was using everything at his disposal. Including her body.

Then Bruna thought of her mother. When she was a child her father had no oxen to pull the plough. Her father strapped the lead reins onto her mother's back and she pulled it. Bruna had passed the sowing months sitting in the grass, watching her mother, barefoot because mud did not destroy feet as it did boots, trudge up and down the wheatfield, driven by her father. When they came in, her father would slump wearily into a chair by the fire, while her mother prepared the food, fed and cared for the children, chickens and rabbits, till he went up to bed. The last thing her mother did every night was clean her father's boots, which he left at the bottom of the stairs for her. In all her years at home, Bruna could not recall her mother ever sitting at the table, sharing a meal with her family. She ate her meals standing, so that she could wait on them. Nor had Bruna ever seen her mother in bed. She rose before and retired after them.

She did all this and much, much more because she believed that if she wasn't needed, her existence was of no value. Bruna knew that her father did not recognise or appreciate her mother's efforts. Her mother did not feel her tiredness was something that had to be acknowledged, anyway. Her sweat, aches and pains were expressions of her love. That was how women gave, thought Bruna. They put everybody's needs ahead of their own. It was how a mother proved her worth.

The cold air gnawed at Bruna's cheeks, chafing them red. She missed her footing on a rock on the road and stumbled, and Artemio caught her. She held baby Pasquale closer to her breast. Like steam in a cold draught, she could feel her new-found peace evaporating.

When they reached Poggio's front door, Bruna turned to Artemio with resignation and acceptance.

Lisa Clifford

'Best you get a boy. If we keep him till he's older, he'll be of more use around the farm.'

11

November

There was a time when the people who travelled from Florence to Stia along the road in front of Campo Alto admired how beautifully the farmhouse blended traditional functionality with natural grace. It was a rustic, two-storey Tuscan farmhouse, with a spacious covered terrace that protected drying produce from the elements. Yet it also had a genteel air that invited you to cast your day aside, sit down, relax and indulge in its views.

But no more.

In November 1906, moss grew like velvet carpet on Campo Alto's roof. It plugged out the rain but wedged in the damp. The chimney's outer tip had collapsed, and on the once-regal terrace, trees fought for space with a chopping block. In the yard, a rusted bedhead, along with cartwheels that had long ago lost their spokes, leant against the wall. A rudimentary outdoor blacksmith's forge was surrounded by a scorched crater. Near it, a cracked millstone, impossible for two, or even four, men to move, sunk clumsily into the uneven earth. Weeds like pond creepers grappled at anything within their reach and they'd snagged an abandoned rabbit cage. Around it, unidentifiable pieces of ancient machinery tinkled in the breeze.

Four months after agreeing to take on Campo Alto, after arriving a little early for his meeting with the *sensale* and Sauro to sort out the tools, Artemio stood at the top of the path that swung onto the back entrance of his new farm, taking in the hoarded junk. His eyes skipped from one dejected object to another as he wondered how it was possible that in the half-dozen years since he'd been to his brother's farm, Campo Alto's house could have fallen into such a shameful state of disrepair.

More shocking to him than anything were the windows. Not one had an intact pane of glass. Some frames were empty; others had panes with holes, as though a fist or a ball had gone straight through them to leave gapes with cracks that fanned out like spider webs. Glass lay in shards below the windows from where it had fallen.

Inside the house, all the *scuri* (wooden shutters with no slats) were closed against the light. With no glass for protection, only the *scuri* separated the house's inhabitants from the wind and the cold. But the thick boards would leave the house in permanent darkness. Like a trapdoor to a cellar, they would have to stay shut. Artemio despaired at the thought of his children. Their chestnut bowling would be played by candlelight. Their sheets would be wet with the damp. The wind would whistle through the sides of the *scuri* like a lost soul.

As though in tune with his thoughts, the breeze picked up and ruffled the side of his jacket's lapel. There was always wind at Campo Alto. It either coaxed or whipped the leaves into noisy confusion. It bent people into submission. Up here the gales blew ice.

Artemio took off his hat and ran his hands through his hair. The cold seeped through his patched jacket and sweater. It collected in the spaces between the woollen stitches. He patted his arms to stamp it out. Beside him, his dogs panted thick air, looking up to him for commands. When he did not move on, they plopped down in the gravel, their tongues lolling like red ribbons from their mouths. He had brought them with him to protect against the wolves said to be roaming the woods around the high farms.

He'd left his chestnuts over their fire in the *seccatoio*; his hair, skin and clothes still reeked of the smoke. Coal smuts marked his cheeks. He slept with them now and would continue to do so for at least the month of November. The fire had to be watched continuously. While he was out today, his hired woman was to stand guard. His final count was fifty *quintali*, five thousand kilos. He'd never amassed such a quantity. When leaving them, he had felt moderately confident that today's negotiations would go well. Now, however, there did not seem much to haggle over.

Shaking his head with disappointment, he looked down at his dogs. At his stare, they rose and loped towards him, hoping for some attention. But Artemio strode past them, decided to check the fields, the pigsty and summer sheep pen from above. From the highest point of the ridge, up a short track, he surveyed Campo Alto's fields with a critical eye. He cursed himself for not doing this months ago, but then, he muttered, it would have made no difference anyway. He would still have taken on this farm; even in its current state of disarray its potential was obvious.

The pastures to the left of the house looked promising but had not been cultivated with care. He could see that the oats, wheat and barley were planted, but there was no indication that the smaller field of wheat and mixed winter broad beans was ready. At Poggio his mixed forage would soon be cut and stored so that when the snow was too high for the animals to graze it could be mixed with the hay. Artemio searched for field ditches, but could not find any. Silvio had already cleaned up their rainwater trenches. Winter rains stagnated and destroyed crops. Runoff was essential. For good measure the boy had also put poisoned wheat grains down the field-mice holes. The man who took over Poggio would be well pleased with the farm's preparation. It would make his first twelve months easy.

Artemio spied the vegetable garden. It was as desolate as the house. The hens' yard had lost some of its fencing. Still, he noticed, the coop's rickety wooden door was well planked against intruders. In the distance, in a fine-looking field further down to his left, a flock of sheep grazed. He counted them out. Forty-five, a lot more than he had anticipated. Artemio did his calculations. He would add his eight to the half-flock left by Sauro (seven he would have to leave behind for the new man); that came to about thirty sheep. One sheep gave almost a litre of milk a day; thirty litres would make two small rounds of pecorino. In their four months of milking, from April to July, that would give him about two hundred and forty rounds to sell and eat for the year. Excellent. He was making only one decent-sized round per day with his flock of fifteen now. *An incredible difference in income at Campo Alto*, he thought, starting to perk up. He would feed the lambs raw potatoes, fatten them up nicely and sell as many as he could. Behind him, Il Villaggio's church bells chimed, a reminder of the time, and Artemio, now feeling remarkably better, wondered why none of Sauro's boys were in the fields, or watching the sheep.

Off the main road, led by the clouds that cast shadows before him, Farm Manager Certini's tiny figure was making its way along the track that led to Campo Alto's barn and house. Certini walked straight into the barn and almost immediately came back out with Sauro and two of his sons. Artemio shielded his eyes and looked along the back track that he had recently walked. The *sensale* was there, using a thick walking stick that could double as a weapon should he need it. He placed it on the ground in measured time with the fall of his right foot. His stride was leisurely, pompous, as though he were out on a Sunday to catch some fresh air, rather than on his way to conduct the transferral of goods between farmers. He wore a black fedora hat and a heavy woollen cloak with a fine suit underneath. Artemio called to his dogs and walked down from the mountain's summit to await the *sensale*'s arrival at the beginning of Campo Alto's back track.

'*Buon giorno*, Signor Sensale,' Artemio greeted dutifully.

'*Buon giorno*, Bruni. Nasty business the other day, but I've put it behind me and know that you have too, eh?' The *sensale* put out his hand. Artemio looked at it suspiciously, then shook it without replying and turned to walk down to the house. The *sensale* matched his pace to Artemio's.

'I must mention better news. I have keen interest in your chestnuts from a Florentine dealer. We will talk about it later, but it seems he is ready to buy all you have, once they are dried and ground.'

Artemio's chestnuts had only ever been sold piecemeal to Casentino men. A sale of most of his full fifty *quintali* would be most financially beneficial.

'I would be interested to hear more, once we have the business of these tools and livestock out of the way,' Artemio answered.

'Marvellous! Now, don't let me leave without discussing it,' the *sensale* responded cordially.

At the sound of their voices, Sauro's two eldest sons descended the steps from the terrace. Artemio looked at them, surprised by how much Giuseppe and Pietro had grown. He hazarded that they were about twenty and eighteen years old respectively. Both had the round, honest face of their mother. She had also given them her high hairline and wide-set eyes. Their thick black hair was Sauro's and so were their lips, which were thinner and more expressive than hers. Artemio was surprised at how pleased he was to see them.

'*Salve*. Hello,' he said with a half-smile.

The boys moved forward silently to shake their uncle's hand, though Artemio sensed a reluctance to do so. Both boys avoided eye contact, and Artemio was fairly sure his brother would have led them to believe only the worst of him. Sauro had always been envious. The resentment had revealed itself the last time he had visited this farm, when their father had given Artemio the rifle.

It was a beautiful, double-barrelled shotgun and the only item of real value that Signor Bruni had possessed to pass on to his sons. More than a metre long, with light, swirly incisions on its handle and trigger, the Bruni gun was a smooth piece of work. It could hit a target up to thirty-five metres away, with almost no kickback. Signor Bruni had called for Artemio to come outside during the confirmation party for

Sauro's youngest son. In the courtyard that Artemio was standing in now, his father had passed his most precious asset onto him, saying that it was Artemio's, to use judiciously. Artemio shook his father's hand and kissed him on both cheeks, pledging to care for it and to pass it on to Primo when the boy was old enough. But the old man's face had fallen when he'd seen Sauro, his younger son, standing behind Artemio. Sauro was shaking with anger and jealousy. He'd said through clenched teeth that the rifle had always been promised to him. Their father had stammered that he could not remember ever doing so. There was a dreadful moment when the accusations hung in the air, as both Sauro and his father waited for Artemio to pass the gun over to his little brother, to keep the peace, to bind the Bruni men in faith and trust. Artemio supposed that he should have relinquished his prize, but he did not. Instead, he thought of his childhood, the thousands of kilos of chestnuts that he had collected and dried by his father's side. The hundreds of hours he'd trod them, then peeled them with his sisters, while Sauro sat inside by the fire, next to his mother, because he was 'sick'. Artemio deserved the gun. It was only fair that he inherited it.

Today, before the assessment of Campo Alto's goods, Sauro's sons looked coldly at their uncle. Artemio knew their loyalty lay with their father and, realising this, Artemio decided not to pursue any familiarity with questions. Subdued, he walked to the barn with the *sensale* to meet the men. He was conscious of Giuseppe and Pietro following behind him.

'Here they are, we have been waiting for you. A good day to you, Signor Sensale and Bruni,' said Certini.

'And a good day to you, Mr Farm Manager,' responded Artemio, aware that from the conclusion of today's appraisal,

Certini would be his new boss. 'When you told me of the farm's availability, you did not mention its condition.'

'An oversight and not an intended one, I assure you. I thought we could take that into account during today's proceedings.'

'But there are no windows on the house, Mr Farm Manager,' insisted Artemio.

'As the man says, Bruni, that will be taken into consideration,' the *sensale* cut in brusquely.

Till that moment Artemio had not been aware of Sauro. He stood with his two youngest sons in the shadows of the barn's half-closed doorway. When Giuseppe and Pietro went to stand with them, one of Sauro's boys snickered. Artemio brought them into focus and waited several seconds for someone to say something. He sharpened his look at Sauro, but Sauro hung back quietly, with his arms folded. His boys were like a protective wall around him. All were taller than their father, even the youngest, Sabatino, who was fourteen years old now and had been eight at the celebration of his First Holy Communion. Standing next to Sabatino was sixteen-year-old Antonio. Artemio scanned the boys' faces, like a teacher trying to work out who was who and which one was the troublemaker. Only Sauro and Sabatino looked him directly in the eye.

'Sauro,' Artemio said finally. 'I see you and your sons are well. It has been many years.'

'You are a busy man, brother. I have heard of your success with your chestnuts and have imagined the attention they demand.' Sauro stayed within the shoulders of his boys while he regarded Artemio. Neither could think of anything more to say.

'Let me see the tools,' Artemio said simply.

Artemio watched as the four boys stepped aside to let Sauro pull open the barn's double doors fully. Artemio allowed the *sensale* to lead the way, then Certini and Sauro, as protocol dictated. He heard the boys fall in behind him. Two intact windows at the barn's rear were covered with a grime so thick that the light, dusky at the entrance, dissolved into nothing inside. Two of the boys went to a workbench to light a couple of lanterns. They held them high, their round glows slicing through grain dust and a thick stench of animal manure. They waited for directions while the men looked around.

Spider webs as thick as spun wool hung off the ceiling beams next to long-forgotten bunches of dried onions. Empty swallows' nests encrusted their corners. The oxen's yoke and grazing muzzles were suspended along the wall. Ropes, chains and cracked leather reins hung off nails below them. Wicker baskets, orchard rakes, brooms and ladders were stacked underneath. Broken chairs, chipped terracotta urns, a wine barrel and a dozen flasks lay nearby. A waxed canvas umbrella hung open like a dead bat.

Artemio walked to the opposite wall, the nails under his boots making no noise on the layer of muck that covered the cobblestones. He indicated for a boy to follow him so as to see better the sickles, pitchforks, shovels and hoes. Some of these tools were handmade, others were fashioned by the blacksmith. Artemio knew the ones hammered on the anvil should belong to him.

The *sensale* told the boys to stand next to Certini, who had upturned a crate to sit on and was resting a big leather ledger on his lap, his ink bottle nearby on the ground. The *sensale* cleared his throat and suggested they get underway. With one palm open towards Artemio and the other towards Sauro, he began.

'This meeting is to estimate Campo Alto's wealth in tools and livestock. I have been appointed by law to adjudicate these proceedings. If either party, namely Sauro Bruni,' he indicated Sauro with a flourish of his hand, 'or Artemio Bruni objects, he must speak during the course of proceedings. No further objections to my rulings will be heard, nor can they be appealed. What is decided today will be signed off today. The secondary contracts that concern your annual gifts to your owner can be certified at a later date.'

Sauro and Artemio each gave one nod to the *sensale* and one to each other.

'Firstly, Sauro Bruni, your departure must be established. Will you vacate Campo Alto by 31 January?'

'I'll leave no earlier than 31 January.'

'And you, Artemio Bruni, will move in 1 February?'

'I will.'

Certini wrote down the dates in his ledger. Artemio watched the portly *sensale* walk to the barn's front corner, where the *treggia*, plough and harrow lay on the ground like medieval torture racks.

'We'll start with the transport and ploughing assets,' he said, looking around at Sauro. 'You made the *treggia*, from the looks of it.'

'Yes,' concurred Certini, 'the farm had no *treggia*.'

'How far down on his dues is Sauro Bruni?' inquired the *sensale*.

Certini ran his finger down the ledger. 'He has to replace the wood that was here upon his arrival. Thirty-six eggs last Easter were not delivered, and he's in arrears four capons – castrated and fattened to two and a half kilos each. Miscellaneous hay and straw also to be replaced from arrival.'

'That's your owner's wood there, that you built that *treggia* with,' said the *sensale*. 'No discussion here. All of this belongs to the farm. Artemio gets the lot.'

Sauro leant back against the wall and eventually nodded.

'Now. The tools. I see there are quite a few home-forged items to add to what came with the farm eleven years ago. Lay everything out for me. Separate what you've made from Campo Alto's assets,' instructed the *sensale*.

Sauro's youngest boys gathered and spread every tool, instrument, utensil, blade and hammer in rows on the ground.

'I made these nails,' said the eldest boy, Giuseppe.

'Damn fine job, young man,' said the *sensale*, bending to pick up and admire each long, quadrilateral, square-headed nail. 'You can keep those, then.'

'And I made that hatchet and the two wide-bladed sickles.'

'I have one hatchet noted and another marked missing. It appears one was misplaced at the time of your tool appropriation in 1895.'

'Yes, I remember,' said Sauro. 'We never found it, so several years ago my son made his own.'

'You are sure you made it?' asked the *sensale*.

'Try to find the blacksmith's stamp,' Sauro interjected with pride.

The *sensale* reached forward and turned over the hatchets. One had the initials *MGP* stamped near the smooth wooden handle, the other a scratchy patch in the same place. He studied them, picked them up and tested their weight by bouncing them in his hands. He turned them upside-down before placing them back on the ground. Rocking back onto the heels of his shoes, he continued to size them up, while his fingertips brushed at the hair that protruded from his nose.

'It is my view that this one's been tampered with,' he announced, pointing to the hatchet with the scratches near the handle.

'With all due respect, Mr Sensale, my son told me he made that one and I believe him.'

'Leave it with me then. I'll take it down to Marco Giovanni Pendini, the smith in Stia. That's his work. I'm guessing your son found this hatchet but is claiming it's his own work.'

Giuseppe studied the *sensale*. 'Sir, I don't want any problems. My uncle can have it.'

'Holy God, boy! You made it, it's yours,' protested Sauro.

'Father, just *leave* it,' the boy said tersely.

Sauro tensed and his eyes widened, but he nodded his assent to the *sensale*.

For the rest of the morning the men worked through every piece of Campo Alto property, of which nothing belonged to Sauro. The wide-bladed sickles Giuseppe had made were passed on to Artemio in lieu of the capon and egg debt. So was every bolt, shear, hook, tong, vice, screwdriver, tomato pole, axe and metre of cord. Each item was accounted for in Certini's ledger and then officially signed off to Artemio. The two-handled saw was also appointed to him, along with the extra rigging for the oxen harness that Sauro claimed he had bought with his own profits in 1899. They would, the *sensale* said, nullify the hay and straw that was provided for him when he originally took over the farm.

Sauro nodded reluctantly. He seemed to want to disagree but lacked the courage. The boys, in their respectful but sullen way, shuffled from one tool to the next, growing incredulous at their losses. But each of them was resigned to it. Everyone knew there was nothing they could do to change the balance of their affairs.

Towards late morning the *sensale* concluded his dealings in the barn and suggested they all move outside to discuss the livestock. Though the day was bleak with the arrival of the clouds, the *sensale* appeared glad of the cold air. The boys trailed behind aimlessly, confirming Artemio's guess that they had been given no direction on the day's work. They sulked a little, kicked dirt and patted Artemio's dogs.

'Fedo! Jordano!' he called, whistling the dogs back to his side. He did not believe in playing with other men's dogs. It spoilt them for work and made them look for attention elsewhere.

The farm manager knelt on the ground and balanced his book on one knee.

'Certini!' yelled the *sensale*. 'Sheep count?'

'Forty-five,' came the call back.

'Twenty-two to Sauro Bruni, twenty-three to Artemio Bruni, along with all the cheese-making utilities,' he said.

Sauro let out a loud gasp. 'But is this fair? Surely after eleven years I should be awarded the extra sheep. Some of those moulds I made myself. You're leaving me with nothing.' His appeal was directed mainly to Certini, who had kept to himself, neatly writing up his numbers along his columns.

'This is business, Sauro,' Certini replied evenly. 'And as much as I'd like to see you leave here with some tools, seeds and plenty of sheep, because God knows you'll need them, this is out of my hands.' Certini leant over his ledger and spat onto the ground. He turned back to his page, not bothering to rub his phlegm into the dirt.

Like a judge preparing to slam down his gavel, the *sensale* declared, 'The division of Campo Alto's wealth is closed!'

Painstakingly, Certini ruled off his page, and then dipped his pen into the ink bottle beside him one more time, before holding it out to Artemio. More than satisfied with his share, Artemio took the offered pen quickly. He crouched before Certini and scrawled his X beside his name.

'Sauro?' Certini queried, proffering his pen. Sauro had his back towards the group, as though he were surveying the mountains before him, but he turned promptly enough and came to add his X beside his brother's. When he brought his head back up, Artemio caught his expression. His eyes were wide, puzzled. But Sauro did not so much as glance in Artemio's direction. He turned on his heel and walked with purpose back to the house, pursued by his gang of boys.

Artemio found himself wishing that his brother had looked him in the eye, just once, before he took off. It was not that he was worried about the estimation; his brother would not need those tools as a *pigionale* in their parents' home. It was better that they remained here. Nor did he feel he should have spoken up in his brother's defence. Sauro had had his chance, now it was his turn. He would just have liked to say goodbye. Who knew when they would see each other again? And they were brothers, after all.

Instead, he turned to Certini, who was standing up, brushing the dirt off his knees. 'What about the window panes?'

'I think you'll agree that today's reckoning has been more than fair towards you?'

Artemio nodded.

'I'll talk to the owner about the glass. That's all I can promise. Good day, Artemio Bruni.' The farm manager secured his ledger under his arm and walked back the way he had come.

Left alone with the *sensale*, Artemio smoothed his moustache and wondered whether he should accompany the important man back to Poggio and Stia. The *sensale* had been generous to him and Artemio was grateful.

'I shouldn't think you and I will have any problems in the future?' the estimator said, peering closely at Artemio's face.

Artemio nodded soberly. He understood now that after the Stia fight and that unfair ruling against him, the *sensale* had repaid any debt he was owed. Or did Artemio now owe the *sensale* a favour, several favours? Artemio did not know. He had never played this game before.

'I shall lunch with my sister at Scarpaccia today,' the *sensale* went on. 'She fries a chicken so well, though rabbit is my preference. Perhaps you could bring me a nice fat one on market day? Skinned? Marvellous! Farewell, Bruni.' And he strolled away.

As Artemio climbed back down the mountain, he realised that the *sensale* had forgotten to talk to him about the Florentine chestnut merchant. Not to worry, he thought, that would keep till market day. He passed several *seccatoios* and appreciatively breathed in their smoke, which had cast a light grey veil through the trees. Like the scent of salt spray in a village by the sea, the smell of chestnut smoke was a part of his life. Thinking of the day's proceedings, Artemio began to whistle one of Bruna's more jolly tunes. After a while he held out his palm. From the sky the first snow of winter had begun to fall. Like white ash, it dusted his hat and shoulders.

12

December

No one was surprised when, on the evening of 19 December 1906, a thief broke into Artemio Bruni's *seccatoio* and tried to make off with his consignment of chestnut flour. It happened some time after Maria, Anna and Fiamma had finished peeling the dried chestnuts. They'd clung to the walls of the barn, their feet strapped into special sandals studded with nails, their legs inside tall barrels of chestnuts, pumping their knees up and down for days that seemed to have no end. Bruna kept their spirits high with singing, conducting them in chestnut folksongs like a maestro before an orchestra.

While the women trod the chestnuts, Artemio sold the pigs, bar the sow and the one fattened for slaughter. Mario and Silvio oversaw the pork butcher's knife when he came to Poggio to slice and mince the fat pig into prosciutto haunches and sausages. The boys held the jug to the squealing pig's throat and caught its blood for *roventini* – blood pancakes with pecorino. They collected the bones for soup and boiled its head for *capaccia* – the freshest of all the salted pork meats. The meat and the chestnuts brought great cheer to the household, as the cheese room was empty except for *conserva*, wheat, beans, polenta, apples, walnuts, black cabbage and one last round of pecorino.

Artemio went to his owner's home to hand over half the slaughtered pig and half his year's cash profits, and to have his Christmas gifts of capons weighed and accepted. Standing in the villa's courtyard, waiting in line with several other farmers, he heard the keys of a pianoforte ripple a Christmas carol. The distant laughter of the owner's wife and children floated on the snowflakes around him. The villa's front door was adorned with tinsel, pretend white doves and a wreath of silver thread and ribbons. Artemio did not wonder what it was like inside the house, past the decorated door. The grandeur of the frescoes and chandeliers that he could see through the windows was well beyond his aspirations. This was his final visit to Poggio's owner and he thought only of Giubbotto's acceptance of his payments and gifts, before he moved on to a new life at Campo Alto.

With his fees paid and the chestnuts peeled, Artemio was free to rig up his oxen and go to the mill to grind the chestnuts into flour. The trip was not far, but it was steep and the going was tough with a fully laden *treggia*. The snow, which had fallen for most of December, made the sled-like wagon slip sideways. When Artemio passed the Madonna shrine on the roadside, he made the sign of the cross and prayed that he would complete the round trip without overturning. Buried in white powder, only the Madonna's face and outstretched hand were visible.

Awaiting their turn to grind, Veleno and Culino were already at the mill, sitting on their sacks of dried chestnuts. They had heard some stories that Artemio had been favoured in the Campo Alto estimation and they were intrigued. At first the men discussed how incoming farmers always received a better deal than outgoing farmers. They said that managers had little to lose by short-changing a man who was leaving and much to gain by shoring up stock with a new man. But what had Artemio to say about such obvious preferential treatment? What was going on, they yelled over the crunching clank of the mill cogs. Artemio refused to answer their questions and both Veleno and Culino were annoyed by his reticence. But there were rumours circulating that his brother had been closed out of discussions, they persisted. Had he nothing to say? Artemio shook his head and changed the subject.

When the mill owner, who in the past had been Artemio's major client and purchaser, offered to buy a healthy portion of Artemio's chestnuts and Artemio refused, the men asked what plans he had for his chestnuts. Artemio replied that the *sensale* had lined him up a Florentine sale. At that, the men fell silent, though Artemio was happy to tell them that the Florentine merchant would come to pay for the chestnut flour and take it away in a matter of days.

Veleno and Culino watched Artemio depart and, after he was gone, angrily muttered between themselves that the *sensale*'s deal was clearly a favour. Bruni had sided with the gentry, they said. He had become too self-important. He was still a *mezzadro*, but was being treated like a landowner or, at the very least, someone who was soon to be one. The men shook their heads, disappointed. They said that Artemio had changed and that he was no longer the man they'd grown up with.

Days later, Artemio awoke past midnight to the sound of frenzied barking from the barn. The dogs had heard wolves, thought Artemio; they were doing their best to rouse him. He rolled off his bed, careful not to wake Bruna and the baby. From the window above the kitchen he eased open the shutter. Grateful for the full moon, he cast his eyes about the field and walnut trees at the top of the track. The land was an undulating white dune with twinkling crystals.

Perceiving movement in the elongated shadows of the house, Artemio saw, only metres away, that a man was bending into his *seccatoio* window. Whoever he was, he had been unable to get in through the locked back door, so had opened the window and was systematically removing the branches over the beams, trying to get down to the floor, where Artemio's chestnut flour was stored in bags stacked high. Payment and collection were due the following day, and Artemio had no doubt that the thief knew this. He was so close to the house that Artemio could almost smell him.

Silently, Artemio slipped downstairs to fetch his rifle. A ray of moonlight lit his way. It helped him pack his gunpowder down into the barrel of the gun. He fumbled with the two lead balls, the adrenalin and the knowledge that he was going to shoot a man making his fingers stiff. Still, he was clear-headed. The chestnuts were his gold, his future. He would not hesitate to kill to save them. Creeping back upstairs he was careful not to creak the wood.

Artemio opened the window a sliver and poked the rifle's barrel out. He hoisted the gun up high and took aim. The crack of the shot blasted through the night. He missed his target, the bullet ricocheting off the stone wall, the sparks making the thief fly off his feet in surprise. But he was on his feet again in an instant, galloping through the knee-high snow, towards the road. Artemio took aim again, steadily, determined to kill the man. The second shot hit the pear tree, the one his family sat under for lunch during wheat harvest. It splintered a branch and made the snow sink to the ground in slow motion. The thief dodged like a deer and hurdled a jutting stone. *He knows the terrain*, thought Artemio. Hitting the ground after the jump, the thief's hat lifted off, making him falter, stop and turn in a low-running crouch to retrieve it.

Artemio gasped. The moon's luminous rays reflected in the man's flame-coloured hair, the copper in it gleaming like rusted iron. The man replaced the hat on his head and paused to catch his breath. Then he stood, edgy but somehow impudent, looking towards the house, as though daring Artemio to shoot again. When Artemio did not fire, the man tipped the brim of his hat in mock salute and jogged leisurely up the road.

The next morning Artemio successfully traded his chestnut flour for money. Obliged to pay Giubbotto the owner's portion, he then journeyed down to Stia to make his payment. There he met Culino, Veleno, Botte and Mestolino at the bar and recounted the previous night's events in detail to them. Bound by a sense of unanimous shock at Il Rosso's blatant thievery, the men sympathised. They concurred that there was no point in confronting Il Rosso, as he would only deny the break-in and would in all likelihood become violent. As there were no witnesses, a complaint to the *carabinieri* was useless. Police involvement would only bring more trouble. Artemio's friends commiserated with him about the shameful lawlessness of his despicable neighbour. Later, when Artemio had left to go home, they mutually agreed that Artemio had had the burglary coming to him.

13

January 1907

It was the absence of sound that woke Artemio on the morning of 3 January 1907. Lying on his back, he opened his eyes, propped himself on his elbows and listened. The silence was so dense, it was as if the house were cocooned in thick layers of wool. Artemio turned his head to look at the windows. A dazzling light came through the upper part of the shutters; the lower half was blacked out, as though someone's shadow were blocking the sun.

Artemio found the baby by his side, secured him with a pillow, then pushed back the covers and climbed out of bed. The skin on his face was darker now than in summer, as though he'd washed in coffee. His tan was broken by rough red patches of wind and sunburn. Standing, he unwrapped the olive-oil-soaked rags that covered his hands. The cold air had split his fingers, turning the cracks along his joints into bloody gashes that froze during the day, only to crack again at night. Old wounds, black scars from last year, burst to become fresh cuts this year. The olive oil went some way to keeping his fingers soft enough to bend.

The night before, he and Bruna had smashed the stalactites of ice above all the beds in the house. It had snowed steadily outside, while inside, their body heat had thawed some of the ice on the roof. The water came through the slate roof tiles and dripped into stalactites. If they were not removed they sometimes cracked onto the sleeping faces below. Artemio looked up at the ceiling again now and could have sworn that it creaked.

Having slept in his clothes, he pulled on his boots and then walked over to open the window. When he tried to push open the shutters, they would not budge. Heaving a shoulder against them, he was able to push them enough to see out.

'Mary, Mother of God,' he heard in a whisper behind him. Bruna was awake and sitting up, cradling the baby in her arms, looking beyond him out the window.

Neither of them had ever seen so much snow. The trees, hedges, jutting stones and chicken coop – all of them had disappeared, buried under a white eiderdown. Only the tips of the taller trees, some of them bent into arches, could be seen. The snow rose past their second-floor bedroom window, its bright winter sparkle blinding.

'Get the fire going, Bruna. I'll check the doors.'

As Bruna fetched a crust of bread and gave it to the baby in the walker that Mario had made for him, she thanked God for their foresight. Over the last three days it had snowed continuously, forcing them to stack plenty of logs in the cheese room, along with many pails of water. To keep the newly hatched chicks warm, Ottavia had put them in the clothes-drying drawer below the fireplace, and the chickens and animals had plenty of hay to nestle and keep warm in, so the family was prepared for this isolation.

Bruna could hear Artemio hurling a shovel against the snow that blocked the front door, then the back door, trying to get out of the house. Before long, he called to her that it was no use. The snow had sealed their exits and it was too heavy and hard to dig through. They were completely snowed in.

Bringing the fire to life, Bruna thought that she didn't mind at all. The thought of staying indoors, with nothing more to do than cook, clean and darn, was a welcome relief. They had food, water and a fire. That was all they needed. They could easily sit it out for a few days, at least till the snow receded a little and they could dig their way out.

When the fire was roaring, the children made their way downstairs for breakfast. They, too, were happy to be snowed in. Bruna made a great pot of steaming chestnut polenta and, after devouring it, Mario, Maria, Fiamma and Silvio settled to a game of cards. Artemio sat gazing into the fire, rubbing olive oil onto his hands. He had taken his boots off and put his feet up near the flames. Bruna thought it was a long time since she'd seen him look so relaxed.

Anna and Ottavia were upstairs at their parents' bedroom window, looking outside and marvelling at the snow. They'd been told to remember what this extraordinary winter looked like, because a fall like this came only once in a lifetime, if at all.

'Mamma,' Anna called down the stairs. 'How come there is no smoke coming out of the Mazzettis' chimney?'

Bruna stopped rinsing the dishes and darted a frightened look at Artemio. He stared back at her. They hurried up the stairs at the same time and jostled with the children for a better view through the window.

'They should have their fire lit, Artemio. There's no reason why they wouldn't light their fire. If they don't have heat …' Bruna looked anxiously towards the Mazzettis' house. Artemio also looked for any sign of activity but the snow had engulfed their house up to the second floor too. All was quiet.

'They're going to freeze to death,' said Bruna.

Artemio sucked in his bottom lip; he turned away from the window and looked around the room.

'Oh, my sainted Mary, we can't even get to them,' Bruna cried.

Artemio spun around and opened the window. He put his head out and yelled. 'SIGNORA MAZZETTI! SIGNOR MAZZETTI! ANSWER US! ARE YOU ALL RIGHT OVER THERE?'

The call echoed clearly across the smooth domes of snow. Bruna, Artemio, Anna and Ottavia watched, waiting for some response, hoping to see a shutter flicker open and a hand wave.

Again Artemio called. 'SIGNORA MAZZETTI! FAUSTA! MARCELLO! WE ARE WORRIED ABOUT YOU. CAN YOU HEAR US?'

The other children walked into the room, wondering what all the fuss was about. The heels of their boots knocked noisily on the wooden floor.

'Shhhh! Be quiet!' Bruna commanded. 'Maybe they're yelling back but we can't hear them.' She thought of the elderly couple's feeble voices and knew no sound would travel through the thick walls of their house. Bruna started to cry.

Ottavia moved closer to her mother and started to cry too. 'Are they dead, mamma?' she asked.

Death in the Mountains

Bruna gave a helpless wail. She had begun to feel the terrible pressure of grief around her heart. Primo's vice, the fist, was spreading its steel fingers. Its grip sucked the air from her lungs. The weight of it spread throughout her body, till the heaviness made her stagger. Maria put her arms around her mother and took her and Ottavia to sit on the bed. Anna shut the window, but continued to stare at the house, praying for a sign of life. Bruna, Maria and Ottavia sat in a huddle, sobbing. When the snow reached this level and there were no flames to warm a body or food, they all knew that death would soon follow.

Artemio continued to watch the house too, but after a while he turned once more to gaze into the bedroom. Suddenly and urgently he took Mario's arm. 'Mario! Hold the bedroom door and lift it up with me.'

Asking no questions, Mario did what he was told and together with his father shoved the door up and off its hinges.

'Open the window! And move back!' Artemio told Fiamma.

When the window was open, Artemio put the door on the sill and inched it forward, over the mound of snow. 'Get my boots, jacket and gloves, Anna.'

By the time Anna returned with her father's clothing, Artemio had the door out the window, balanced on the snow.

'Silvio and Mario. Go and get every door in the house.' When the boys understood Artemio's idea, they bolted. From room to room they ran, heaving and pushing doors up and out of their frames, through the window to Artemio, who stood on them outside, balancing like a tightrope walker. Slowly and carefully, Artemio laid the doors out and over the snow, top to bottom, flat like dominoes, so that when he'd finished they resembled a gigantic slippery dip.

Standing below the house on the last one, Artemio waved to the faces smiling encouragingly down at him. 'Come on, Mario; put your coat on. Slide down. We're going to the Mazzettis'!'

'But it's freezing and the snow's too deep. It's over our heads,' Mario called back.

'One door at a time and we'll make it.'

From where he was standing, Artemio could see Bruna's expression change from hopeful anticipation to disappointment in her son. She clutched at Mario, telling him almost incoherently that the Mazzettis had saved their lives more times than she could count and now it was their turn to save theirs.

Mario moved out of Artemio's view and returned with his jacket on. He slid unsteadily down the doors, till he stood next to Artemio. Together, they picked up the door behind them and put it in front of the door that they were standing on. They repeated this all the way down the track, metre by metre, till they rounded the bend on the road that led to the Mazzettis' house.

Bruna watched them till they were out of sight, then led the children downstairs to wait.

Artemio and Mario did not return home that night. They dug through enough of the powdery snow on the Mazzettis' lintel to be able to slide through a small tunnel, dropping onto their feet to push open the front door. After searching the kitchen, the Bruni men found Signora and Signor Mazzetti holding on to each other in bed, asleep. Their lips were purple with cold, their hands white from lack of circulation. Mario said later that he thought they had already passed into paradise, as they were very difficult to wake. He said their faces were beautiful, peaceful, as if they were with angels and did not want to return at the sound of his insistent, earthly voice.

The Brunis found some wood, made a fire and put the coals into two terracotta pots. They wrapped the pots in towels and slipped them into bed with the Mazzettis, while they rubbed their hands and coaxed them back into the world. Eventually the Mazzettis kept their eyes open long enough to explain that they'd finished their wood and Signor Mazzetti had not had the strength to cut any more. They went to bed, they said, knowing that they might never wake up.

A hot broth of watery chestnut polenta with grated pecorino cheese revived the Mazzettis enough to see them out of bed and down onto the stools inside the fireplace. It was too late to attempt the one-kilometre trip to Poggio, so although they knew that Bruna would be worried to distraction, Artemio and Mario stayed the night at the Ospita.

The next morning, they bundled the elderly couple up and carried them back to Poggio. After ten days or so the snow receded enough for the Mazzettis to return home. But Maria went with them, to cut and stack their wood, collect their water and cook their meals.

The news of Artemio Bruni's grand scheme to save the Mazzettis spread throughout the homes of Il Villaggio. People went to *veglia* in those days solely to tell others of the Bruni idea to use doors to escape from a buried home. That Artemio had freed the stranded old couple with such ingenuity, they said, showed how clever the Poggio farmer really was. What a courageous man, they praised, and strong too. When word of the rescue was passed on to Artemio's close friends, Culino, Botte, Veleno and Mestolino, they agreed that while Artemio had recently shown arrogance, and even unseemly ambition, he was actually a remarkably intelligent man. In this way, Artemio earnt the respect and admiration of his fellow farmers and their families. They looked up to him and thought that he was a fine member of their community.

Two weeks after saving the Mazzettis, Artemio Bruni was murdered. He was forty-four years old.

14

On 1 February 1907 Bruna Bruni was required by law to honour her husband's contract and move into Campo Alto. She did so, with only her seven children to help her. Artemio's mother and father decided not to join her after all. They elected instead to stay on in their one-room house at Omomorto, to care for their son Sauro, his four boys and his wife, Amabile. Sauro was their only living son now, they told Bruna, and really they should stay home and help him. So Bruna was left alone, to farm Campo Alto on her own.

One can only imagine how frightened she must have been in the days following the murder of her husband. Yet she demonstrated incredible strength – physical, spiritual and mental – by relocating her family and animals through the snow, up to a new farm with no windows. All this while she must have been feeling a deep sense of abandonment and rejection that Artemio's parents had opted to help Sauro and not her. The exhaustion she suffered while Artemio was alive would have been nothing compared with the harshness of her life after his death. She had to eke their food from the earth, spin their wool and hemp, sew all of their clothes, make their shoes, pay their masters and sell their produce. Moving her own parents up to Campo Alto had never been a consideration. They were too elderly and would have been yet another burden on Bruna.

All that and her sorrow. She was forty years old when her husband was stolen from her, with many years ahead to live without him. Though he was dominant and distant, Bruna loved Artemio. He was the father of her children, the male protector and the authority figure of their household, in keeping with the social norms of those times. She must have felt the loss of his protection and companionship deeply. So why did she do nothing about seeing her husband's killer found, tried and sentenced? Surely she must have wanted his murderer caught and jailed?

Over the following three decades, till at least 1947, Bruna was known as the widow of the murdered man. Wherever she went, she carried that stigma. Even so, and despite her enormous struggles, her small business became a success. Her 'Campo Alto ricotta and pecorino' were much sought after and, in the end, she was recognised for making some of the finest sheep's cheese in Casentino. The profits from her efforts she continued to save carefully, adding them to the money from Artemio's chestnuts that was still hidden in her secret shift pocket. Illiterate as she was, though, Bruna did not know what to do with her earnings. Without her husband, she did not want to buy a farm of her own. She thought it best to give her money to someone to invest for her. Ultimately, she gave her life's savings to the owner of Campo Alto, in the hope that he would keep it safe and make it grow for her. Years later, when she finally plucked up the courage to ask the owner whether her savings had matured, he said that he did not remember her passing on any of her finances. Bruna never saw her money again.

Epilogue

Florence

When I first visited Florence in 1979, I was sixteen years old and fresh out of a Sydney convent. My reasons for travelling at such a young age were not so much to understand Renaissance art or to investigate fine Italian food and wine as to avoid the embarrassment of failing my final school exams. I intended to study Italian and immerse myself in another culture for a couple of years, then go back home when all the exam fuss was over.

Never in my wildest dreams, as I watched my step on the suicidally thin strips of footpath, did I think that one day I would marry one of the boys on the Vespas that shot up and down the tiny streets of Florence. Both my parents had warned me not to fall in love with an Italian, but I couldn't help it – I lost my head over a Florentine. By then I was seventeen years old. However, rather than jump straight into marriage, my

Italian boyfriend and I spent the next eighteen years travelling between Sydney and Florence, trying to decide who was going to leave their home and relocate permanently.

During this time, in the years before we married, when helmets were not yet compulsory and life was a round of hair-whipping motorbike rides to cafés and trattorias in the countryside, we lived with my boyfriend's parents. In those days, de-facto relationships between fiancées and future parents-in-law were not so unusual. My boyfriend was a student and I was a shop assistant, so we couldn't afford a decent Florentine apartment. Also, on the whole, my fiancé's Italian mother preferred to keep her only son (and her only child) at home for as long as possible. I was too young and ignorant to take proper care of her boy. The arrangement suited me fine. My future mother- and father-in-law were incredibly warm and generous. They let my boyfriend and me sleep in till all hours, called us twice a day to a table laden with delicious meals, and all my washing and ironing miraculously appeared folded on a chair next to our bed. Their expectations of me in return for their hospitality were nonexistent. They were happy that we were happy. They embraced me unceremoniously and unpretentiously as the daughter they never had.

For the sake of the anonymity that this story demands, I will call my boyfriend's parents Nonno and Nonna (Grandpa and Grandma), which is what my children call their grandparents today.

Nonno and Nonna were good-natured, simple people from a little-known area in eastern Tuscany, north of Arezzo, called Casentino. They moved to Florence in search of work when they were twenty-three and twenty-one years old respectively, after they were married. Nonno described his birthplace by saying: 'There are no olive trees for oil or grapes for wine where we come from. Forget the Tuscany you know down here in Florence. Our world is completely different.' He had this kind of love-scorn relationship with Casentino. 'We were poor. Always hungry. The Casentinese had empty bellies most of the time. But did you know that's where St Francis of Assisi received his stigmata? The monks and saints built all their sanctuaries on our mountain peaks. You can see a castle from almost every bend in the road.'

Nonno was born in a tiny village at the start of the Casentino ranges. He was a gruff, hard man, who started smoking at nine years old because that's when he started working – driving a pair of oxen, delivering wine between villages, often coming home long after dark. To keep him from falling asleep at the reins, his boss taught him how to smoke. By the time he was eighteen, he was on two packs a day. Nonno was stern but at the same time he loved a glass of wine and a good joke. He said his own father enjoyed a laugh too, but over the years the toughness of his Casentino life knocked the humour out of him.

Like her husband, Nonna is uncomplicated. But unlike Nonno, she was raised on a small, isolated farm about ten kilometres beyond his village. The farm did not belong to her family, she explained, it was owned by a *padrone* – a master; her family farmed it under the *mezzadria* system. That meant that from the time she and her sisters were four years old, they tended the sheep, pigs, chickens, orchard and vegetable garden. Nonna went to school only till second grade, as she was needed too much on the land. In any case, she said, her teacher did not encourage her to stay on. She was a waste of his time. Everyone knew that *mezzadro* children never became scholars.

The farm behind her, life nowadays for Nonna is all about food. It is difficult to stress just how much her mornings and afternoons revolve around cooking. In the days when I first met her, Nonna would start cooking either immediately upon rising or after her return from the markets and bakery – at about eleven in the morning. A beef stew, a bolognese sauce, some homemade potato gnocchi or ravioli: Nonna would always have some dish on the go, so that at one in the afternoon *exactly*, lunch was ready to serve to her family. If it was not, Nonno would be quite cross with her.

As a result, Nonna is nervous under two circumstances. The first is when it's five minutes past one and lunch is not ready. It is her responsibility to produce a good three-course meal twice a day. Cooking is her duty and its obligation was implicit in every part of the way she was brought up. And her meals have to be very tasty too, no excuses, otherwise her husband and son would complain loudly. Still, watching her bustle confidently and diligently in front of the stove top, I realise that it is cooking that gives Nonna her sense of self-worth. Having her men content and satisfied at the table makes Nonna happy. When I would ask why her husband and son never lifted a finger to help, she would say, 'I won't let them. This is my job. I'd be of no use if I didn't cook.'

The second circumstance under which Nonna would become strained was when one of her men discovered her sitting idly on the couch. If Nonno arrived home suddenly and surprised Nonna doing nothing, she would immediately jump up and pretend to be busy. She'd grab a pot or a tea towel, or start folding something, as though she couldn't possibly have let him catch her relaxing. Nonna says that's because a good woman is always active in the home, ready to serve. Nonna was submissive to her husband, yet at the same time not at all malleable. Nonno was the head of the family, but Nonna pulled all the strings.

Many years before I met their son, Nonno and Nonna bought the land around Nonna's old *mezzadro* farm. They built their own house, a two-storey Tuscan-style farmhouse, on the site of the former pigpen and barn. Nonna's sister bought their old *mezzadro* farmhouse. In this way, the Bruni sisters were able to buy out their *padrone*. Once I moved into their place in Florence, going to their holiday home in Casentino became a regular weekend pasttime.

Here in Nonna's country kitchen, under the pretence of having me lend a hand (she was really teaching me how to take care of her son), Nonna taught me how to cook. Together we prepared typically Casentino meals that were shaped by the forests and fields around us. Wild-boar prosciutto for antipasto, then homemade *tortelli* pasta stuffed with spicy mashed potatoes, topped with wild-mushroom sauce. That was often followed by roasted rabbit, pheasant or chicken. Or flattened turkey breast rolled up with a paper-thin omelette and slices of mortadella then pot-roasted with garlic, sage and rosemary. Most of the ingredients heaped onto the kitchen workbench had been lugged there by Nonno. He grew all his own vegetables and bred his own fowl.

Looking back, I realise that it was during these moments in the Casentino kitchen that Nonna first started to tell me of her family history. Both the cooking and the sharing of her stories gave her a sense of passing something on. So I listened, surprised by her tales of empty bellies, wicked managers and jealous neighbours. The life she described was so different from what I had imagined in such a bewitchingly lovely part of the world. But then I understood that I, too, had fallen victim to the collective ignorance about rural Tuscany's past wretchedness because of how the international community reveres what has come from it. The earthy furniture, colours and textures of the rustic farmhouses, which everyone now wants to own and restore, are reproduced in interior magazines and are sought after by designers and homemakers. Our image of Tuscany today is one of extraordinary beauty. Few understand how poor the Tuscans really were. The world's worship of Tuscany as a luxury European destination made it hard for me to reconcile Nonna's anecdotes about her mother's struggle to keep her children fed.

When the refectory table that ran the length of the fire was laid and the shadows of our hands and profiles flickered along the wall behind us, Nonno would pick up on Nonna's tales and add his own flourishes. It was as though the flames, mountain air and local food enticed the family secrets from their hiding places. These were special moments that were far more intimate than our meals in the city. I was a foreigner and knew nothing of their background or how, as Italians, they reacted and reasoned, so Nonna and Nonno explained everything in detail. Nonna especially adored talking about how she grew up. When she was a child the way of cooking, farming, housing and birthing had virtually remained unchanged for the previous five hundred years. As a young girl, Nonna and her six sisters stayed within the confines of their farm, knowing only their immediate neighbours. Their joys were Christmas or Easter lunches, church parades or feasts. The celebrations were held during the day because they had no electricity and returning home at night was treacherous because of the rocky pathways that were their roads. Nonna walked everywhere or travelled on donkeys or by carts pulled by oxen. Every day and all day was work and everyone did their measure for their size. Even if she had

Death in the Mountains

wanted to stay on at school, it would not have been allowed, as every member had to contribute to the survival of the family. It was fascinating stuff and so very, very different from my own Anglo-Saxon heritage.

When talking through her memories, sometimes Nonna was sorrowful, at other times she was regretful; mostly, though, her memories made her smile. And smile she should! It is impossible to ignore the incredible changes in her world since she was a girl on a feudal farm. How many generations can say that they were born in the medieval age and will die in the computer age?

You see, Nonna's father was Silvio, the son of Artemio and Bruna Bruni. Nonna still uses many of the expressions from her father's era, such as *veglia*, *treggia* and *seccatoio*. She calls the shed in our city backyard *la casetta* (little house in the woods) and a baby's stroller *caretto* (old cart pushed like a wheelbarrow). They're words you no longer hear in daily Italian life. They're also words not often found in today's dictionaries, which means Nonna is sometimes difficult to understand. Not only does Nonna use Silvio's vocabulary, she recounts his stories. She says her father often told a story that illustrated how dumb the townspeople thought the farmers were. It's called 'The Donkey That Drank the Moon' and it's about a little Casentino shepherd boy who was sent into the farmyard to give the family's donkey a drink of water. As the boy set the bucket in front of the donkey, he noticed the moon's reflection and thought that the moon had jumped into the water. As the donkey drank, the moon disappeared. Terrified, the child ran to his parents calling, 'Help, help, the donkey has drunk the moon. Now what will we use to light our way at night?' The Florentine people mocked the Casentino farmers with this story. They also used the poorer children among them as domestic workers. Nonna and her many sisters were sent to work as maids in Florence or Rome at eleven or twelve years old.

Silvio Bruni, unlike his sisters, Maria, Anna, Fiamma and Ottavia, and brother Pasquale, never left the land. He married Nonna's petite, blue-eyed mother and stayed on in Casentino to farm under the *mezzadria* system. Silvio died before the Italian government finally abolished the practice of share-cropping in 1982. Old black-and-white photographs of him show a man so upright and grim as to be almost frightening. As Silvio aged, he refused to wear false teeth, so his lips were always puckered into his face, making his mouth turn down. In the photos his eyes are hard, like coffee beans, and his chin is lifted proudly. Nonna says she cannot recall him ever laughing.

Hidden away among all these tales was Silvio's mother, Bruna. From the first moment I heard of Bruna, I was fascinated. Her life was heart-wrenching. When Nonna spoke of her grandparents, I was shocked not only that her grandfather had been murdered, but that no one in her family knew who had killed him or why. The circumstances surrounding the killing did not make sense. How strange that someone could be beaten to death in their own barn and no questions ever asked or answered. How incredibly hard for Bruna to battle on alone, with so many children and a desolate farm to restore. Whenever Bruna's name was mentioned, voices lowered in respect and heads shook with disbelief. 'She suffered such tragedy, that woman. Like iron, she was,' Nonna said about her grandmother. But while my boyfriend's family seemed to accept the story as 'the way things were', I kept fighting a strong sense of injustice. I tried to imagine Bruna and Artemio, did my best to fathom the killer's motive. What had Artemio

Death in the Mountains

done to deserve such a death? Nonna's usual response to my questions was 'Life was cheap in Tuscany then.'

'What did your father say about his father's murder?' I pushed.

'My father refused to talk about it. People gossiped about the whys and hows of the killing behind his back, as though Grandpa Artemio was some kind of criminal involved in a deal gone bad.' Nonna gave a short derisive laugh, then folded her arms and went on. 'My father was ashamed of the whole matter. Men were men then. They did not sit around discussing their inner thoughts and feelings about why their father was murdered.'

'What about Maria, Anna or Mario? Didn't they want to know why their father was killed?'

'They were all ashamed. Everyone just wanted to forget about it.'

I couldn't help feeling even more sorry for Bruna. Her children were too embarrassed to delve into their father's murder, so the family secret remained a rarely mentioned mystery.

When Nonno died of lung cancer, my fiancé and I were jolted out of our indecision and I left Australia permanently, finally moving to Italy after almost two decades of oscillating between the two countries. Within one year of Nonno's death we were married and had our first baby. Our second followed shortly afterwards. The children shifted the family focus from the dead to the living. Our days were full and fast-paced, till the children grew up and life started to slow down once more.

Throughout those baby years, Nonna lived down the road from us in Florence, continuing to travel up to Casentino to visit her family and stay in her holiday house. One night, when out dancing the waltz in Stia, she met another man, a widower farmer who lived only ten kilometres from her own mountain home. Ultimately she married him, a move that took great courage in a society where remarriage is, at best, discouraged (a woman loses her dead husband's pension), and at worst, deeply frowned upon. Nonna's new romance and her permanent relocation up to Casentino saw her accused of abandoning her Florentine family. She weathered the criticism by ignoring it. And by fluttering and twittering around her new husband like a brightly coloured lovebird.

After her remarriage, Nonna's focus shifted onto her husband and away from her grandchildren, which stopped her from being a typical Italian grandma. This put us on an equal footing because I am not a typical Italian daughter-in-law. Sometimes, I know, this disappoints her. There is no doubt in my mind that Nonna would have liked her son to marry an Italian so that she could have had a real Italian daughter-in-law. A girl who did not break into a foreign language when speaking to her grandchildren, making her feel marginalised in her own son's home. Someone who did not complain about the bad-mannered queue jumping and crazy driving but took these everyday hassles in her chic Italian stride. A daughter-in-law who did not question her servile attitude towards her new husband and her son. Having said that, and having been a part of her family for thirty years, I know that Nonna loves me very much and (I think) would not swap me for a compatriot now.

I do try to make up for my foreign, feminist ways by always being polite and listening to Nonna talk. And talk is something Nonna does incessantly now. The older she gets – she's eighty – the more her thoughts tend to dwell on the past. Thankfully, that's a subject I find extremely interesting.

Whether her reminiscences include Grandma Bruna's oft-repeated sayings or an ancient family recipe, Nonna's family history never fails to draw me in. I hear about the past more than ever now that Nonna has moved into her new husband's home and transferred responsibility for her Casentino holiday house over to me. Our positions are reversed, as she is the guest and visits for lunch or dinner. Now she helps me in the kitchen and I oversee the property's fruit and chestnut harvests. It's up to me to make sure the children collect the water from the well, pick the seeds out of the tomatoes for next year's crop and gather the walnuts before they are destroyed by the rain or the wild boars.

I remember one particular day, not long after the funeral of one of Nonna's sisters, when I felt my connection with the Bruni family change. Four of the remaining five Bruni sisters had come to our house for lunch, all of them sad, each armed with a basket of chestnuts. I realised, then, that this age-old nut, the food that had kept so much of Europe alive throughout its winters, was the women's comfort food. The sisters explained that it was not only the chestnut, but its preparation, its smell as it roasted over the fire, the final process of sharing, peeling and eating it, that comforted them so profoundly. They talked sadly about its demise.

'The roads are full of them, especially down at Poggio,' said one sister. 'They're piled high along the road's shoulder.'

'They run over them, mush them,' Nonna added, pursing her lips. 'The men don't clear the forests like they used to. They have so much to eat that the chestnuts are forgotten. They fall down onto the road and the men *leave* them there!'

'It's the cancer,' another sister added. 'The chestnut trees have a cancer now. It is rotting them from the inside and no one knows how to cure them.

'They say,' she went on, 'that if this disease had taken hold one hundred years ago, there would be half as many Tuscans as there are today. Whole families would have died of starvation. The tree doctors say they are doing what they can. But in my opinion they are dying from lack of love. The younger people don't care about them like we do.'

Nonna put her nose up and sniffed the odour of charred wood as the chestnuts began to crackle in the pan. 'Goodness, how Grandpa Artemio loved his chestnuts.'

I asked if any of Artemio's children had inherited his gift with them. The Bruni sisters said no, most had swapped country life for the city. But their father, Silvio, had worked with them.

Mario Bruni, Silvio's elder brother, had always wanted to move down to Florence, they said. He never did, though. After Artemio was murdered, Mario stayed on in the mountains. He remained loyal to his mother, although he was a drunk and his drinking increased till he was eventually known as a bitter, violent man.

Maria was always beautiful, always desired, the Bruni sisters said, but she never married. In a courageous move that surprised all who knew her, she left her mother and was the first of all her siblings to move to Florence. Maria found work as a chambermaid in a big international hotel and eventually became head of housekeeping. Throughout her life Maria was courted only by bold men. But they were materialistic braggarts, always overbearing. They were the kind of men who felt they deserved her as a prize. She rejected each of her suitors, saying she was never approached by someone she could love.

Fiamma eventually left Campo Alto for Stia. She found work in the textile factory and married a man from the nearby steelworks. Anna met and married a Casentino farmer who decided to try his luck in the city. They moved down to Florence, where Anna's husband became a pastry chef and did well, eventually buying his own café. After some years, Ottavia went to stay with Anna, as Maria had found her a maid's job in her hotel. Baby Pasquale grew into a big man and he, too, left Campo Alto, so only Bruna and Mario remained. Pasquale moved to Florence and worked as a manual labourer, sometimes beside Nonna's husband. Apparently, Nonno and baby Pasquale became quite close.

While absorbing the fates of the sisters' aunts and uncles, the idle interest that I had always felt towards the old Bruni clan changed. All at once I became aware of a real affection for them. Their losses, their pain, actually meant something. It was peculiar: to belong to a country and family only through marriage, yet to feel such a strong link with their dead.

During the months that followed, I began to research the lives of Tuscan farmers a century ago to get a better understanding of how the family had lived. Very few publications described their daily routines and seasonal agricultural work; the best accounts were in self-published books, written by the descendants of farmers. These descendants had, like me, realised that when the last of Nonna's generation passes away, so will all the knowledge of the old rural ways. I started to interview local farmers, priests and social archivists. Obviously there were no diaries or letters to chase up.

'We all grew up with *that* story. It was the local folklore around here,' Il Villaggio residents told me. Then they'd pass on the gossip they'd heard. Each new snippet made my heart race. Could I seriously discover the identity and motive of Artemio's killer, one hundred years after the crime was committed? Then the search shifted its direction and I began to care less about who had actually wielded the weapon and why. As I spoke to the old people, indentifying the murderer became less important than passing on the Bruni stories. This is a story about a family, and the members of that tightly knit group had personalities with voices. Those voices spoke to me through old ladies in shawls by fireplaces in the house down the road or through Bruna's brass polenta pot, still on our mantlepiece in the mountains. The sound of the Bruni songs seemed to echo through the woods while I collected chestnuts in the same time-honoured way as they had. Their voices resonated through Poggio, which lies abandoned, but just as rock solid as when it was built six hundred years ago, the essence and mood of the house very much intact, the hearts of its past inhabitants pulsing in the rocks that form its walls. Making the Brunis come to life was not too hard after I'd seen their tools, connected with their nature and walked through their house.

By 2006 I realised that I had so many stories and such vivid imagery in my head that I had to put it all down in a book. I felt it was time to ask Nonna whether she would mind if I wrote a book about her grandparents, Artemio and Bruna. I felt that I was facing a strong family moral dilemma: I was poking my nose in where it did not belong. I was being what the Italians call an *opportunista*. Although everyone seemed comfortable enough with my questions, sometimes I felt that I was trespassing on territory that was better left unexplored. What right did I have to go around opening old wounds? I could not proceed with my inquiries if my husband's family did not want me to. But Nonna said that an investigation into her grandparents' lives and the criminal offence against them did not trouble her. She doubted that it would worry or hurt any of her sisters either. She would, in fact, like to know who was behind the killing and would help me track down the Brunis' grandchildren to interview. We should start, I said, by finding out some firm dates.

'When was your grandfather killed? Do you know the exact date?' I asked.

'I'm not sure, but I can call my sister. I think she remembers,' replied Nonna.

Ever since I married my husband, we seem to have encountered odd coincidences with dates. Our first baby was born on Nonno's birthday and our second on Nonno's brother's birthday. Nonno died on my birthday. Despite this strange synchronicity with dates, I was surprised when Nonna came back to me on the question of the exact date of Artemio's murder.

'My sister told me Grandpa Artemio died on 17 January 1907,' Nonna said a few nights later as we prepared dinner together in my kitchen.

'Wow, almost one hundred years ago,' I said.

'What's the date today?' Nonna asked, grabbing my arm.

I looked at the calendar. 'My goodness! That's today. Grandpa Artemio died exactly ninety-nine years ago *today*.'

We looked at each other and giggled nervously, the hairs on the backs of our necks prickling. It was at that moment that I knew I had to write this book. I had the most uncanny feeling that, eventually, I would find out who killed Artemio Bruni.

The elderly gentleman in front of me had tubes that ran from his nose to a mobile oxygen cylinder. He pulled the cylinder on a little trolley behind him, and after he had greeted me at his front door, he seemed only just to make it to his chair at the kitchen table before his energy expired. Juggling his tubes and his trolley, he sat down slowly, with a grateful sigh.

As thin and old and sick as he was, his eyes were clear. Like shiny brown pennies, no cloud or fog in them. Everyone had said that he had a keen mind and a good memory. Judging from his expression, they were correct – he was sharp, all right. In his younger years he would have been a confident man, and from the direct way he had of staring straight into my eyes, maybe even a lady's man. He had probably been good-looking too, in that strong, self-assured way of Italian men.

Nonna had brought me to see Giorgio because he was Anna's son. When Bruna lost her life's savings to the owners of Campo Alto, she gave up the cheese-making business and moved down to Florence, where she could be cared for by Anna, her favourite child and the one who nursed her in her final years. In Italy people tend to die at home; only the very sick or very rich are placed in hospitals or nursing homes. As a rule, children take their parents in, so that they can pass away in peace surrounded by family.

For the last five years of her life, Bruna had lived with Giorgio and his family and he had come to know his grandmother well. If anyone was likely to hold the key to the mystery it was Giorgio.

Driving there, to Giorgio's apartment on the outskirts of Florence, where rows of beige terrace houses crammed grid-like streets and cars fought people for space, I had told Nonna how much weight I'd attached to this meeting. As her monologue, 'Giorgio was the eldest child, he worked in a chicken battery for years …' had trilled on, I'd nodded distractedly, trying to second-guess what kind of a man this cousin was. My greatest concern was that he would be offended by my questions. He could accuse me of prying; he might be angry because of that. Then again, Nonna had said he was a nice man. Perhaps with some gentle coaxing he would tell me what he knew of his grandparents.

I was terribly nervous. I'd talked to everybody. My investigation had lasted three years and this was the end of the trail. If Giorgio, with his sparky memory and proximity to the dying Bruna, was not the secret's keeper, I had nowhere left to look. Yet even if he did know who the murderer was, he might simply decide not to tell me, and I would have no choice but to accept that. Keeping the one-hundred-year-old family secret was his choice, and his alone.

At first our conversation roamed around Bruna's last years. It was good to hear that she had died peacefully in her sleep one afternoon. She'd been sitting by the fire, snoozing, and everyone had tiptoed around, not wanting to disturb her, not realising that she was dead. No, Giorgio said, Bruna did not talk much towards the end of her life – though she often mentioned the Mazzettis.

'After Signor Mazzetti died, Signora Mazzetti would go and stay with her up at Campo Alto. Bruna was with Signora Mazzetti when she died. They left their house to the Catholic Church. Childless couples used to do that. It bought their indulgence, their ticket to heaven. The Mazzettis died knowing their place in paradise was assured,' Giorgio said.

I steered the talk towards Artemio by saying that Pratovecchio's council had Artemio's death certificate. (Years earlier the town had absorbed the little village of Stia into its jurisdiction.) The date of his death was recorded as 20 January, three days after the date that I had been given. It had been reported by a man named Felice.

'Yes, that'd be right,' Giorgio agreed, amicably enough. 'Felice would not have gone immediately to report it. He probably stayed on with Bruna for a day or two then travelled down to Stia. She would have needed help. Council would have just listed the day of death on the day that it had been reported.'

'But the death certificate had his cause of death listed only as a head injury, not that he'd been beaten to death.'

Giorgio absently tapped his teeth with his teaspoon. 'I know where they buried him,' he said, as though talking to himself. 'It's that cross down by the stream behind Poggio. It marks his grave. They kept his body in the bedroom till they had to move it into the barn, where it stayed for three weeks. When they moved him, his hair had frozen onto his pillow and they had to snip it off with scissors. They couldn't bury him sooner because they could not dig a pit for the coffin. The ground was ice, frozen solid.'

Nonna and I waited for him to go on. He did not.

'Giorgio,' I said gently, 'Il Rosso, the Brunis' neighbour, seemed to delight in antagonising Artemio – perhaps that got out of hand. Do you think that may have been possible?'

Giorgio opened his mouth to speak, but Nonna interrupted. 'For most of my life I heard that Grandpa Artemio and Il Rosso had a big fight at the Stia markets. That day he said he was like a match that would explode and cause trouble. We were always under the impression that he carried out his threat.'

'I'd heard that too,' said Giorgio. 'And that if Il Rosso was ever accused of the murder, he would not deny it.'

'My feelings were that he never really had enough of a motive to kill,' I said, pushing a wave of disappointment away because it seemed that Giorgio was only dealing in theories, just like everyone else.

'Il Rosso used the Stia fight to gain a reputation as a fearless man. He did not deny slaying my grandfather because being known as a murderer gave him distinction.'

'What a horrible man,' said Nonna.

Giorgio nodded at her, then, with a surprisingly swift change of focus, turned to face me. 'Why is it that you want to know so badly who killed my grandfather?'

'I am intrigued by how someone can be murdered and nothing be done,' I explained, conscious that my defence had better be good. 'I'm angry for Bruna that she had such a hard life and never saw justice. Another thing too – having discovered so much about Bruna, I have found that I really like her. I feel as though I know her and as if by knowing her I owe her something. You could even say that I have grown to love her. She was such a good, strong woman. But why did she just sit back and do nothing?'

'My grandmother was a much better woman than you,' Giorgio said, looking very serious.

'I don't doubt that for a minute,' I responded quickly, feeling somewhat taken aback. 'But was she a good woman because she forgave her husband's killers and therefore let them go? Is that a good woman? One who forgives and forgets?'

'Who knows if she ever *forgave* them? I don't!' Giorgio answered heatedly. 'I do know, though, that she never ever *forgot* them. The difference between you and Bruna is that you expect society to pay for any injustice done to you. You believe that a judge, a jury and an executioner will do your punishing for you. Bruna believed that God was the punisher. She knew the Almighty would see justice done, in His way, in His time. The Church and its ideals were all she knew. She may not always have got the Church's message right, what with all the sermons and prayers in Latin, but with her superstitions and religious faith, it was the only part of society outside her small community that she trusted.' Giorgio's Tuscan accent became thicker the more agitated he became.

'You mean your grandmother trusted to divine justice?'

'I mean she had complete faith in God's law of nature. *That* law was the only law that mattered to her and it would see that the killers paid a price for taking her husband.

'Bruna also had the grace,' Giorgio went on, lowering his voice, calming down a little, 'never to tell others who murdered Artemio – especially Mario. A full-scale family war would have broken out if she had and she could not have borne that. Protecting her family was her priority. She only told my mother, Anna, and my mother told me.'

Giorgio paused and we stared at each other. He knew. Giorgio was the keeper of the secret. Looking at him, I felt an overwhelming relief. Thank God someone knew. Oddly, that relief was coupled with an unwillingness to ask him directly who the killer was. After all my effort, now that the answer to the mystery was finally within my reach, kept by the fragile old gentleman opposite me, any regret or unease he might suffer in divulging was no longer worth it.

'Would you believe it if I told you that nobody, to this day, has ever asked me who took my grandfather's life?'

I nodded and said that although that would be surprising, I would believe it. 'What is important to one person means nothing to another,' I said.

Giorgio slowly looked at Nonna, then at me. I returned his gaze with gravity and something passed between us. It was as if Giorgio had decided to bestow something upon me, and in that moment his spirit gave it to mine.

'It was Sauro's boys.'

'Sauro's boys? They killed Artemio?' Out of the corner of my eye I saw Nonna raise her hand and cover her mouth.

'No!' she uttered.

'They did. The eldest three. Giuseppe, Pietro and Antonio.'

I was absolutely stunned at this revelation and so was Nonna. So many different people had accused Il Rosso, Giubbotto, Sauro, even Mario. The three of us sat in silence, thinking about the implications of Artemio's own nephews bashing him to death.

'Oh, sure,' Giorgio went on, with a deep breath through his nose and his oxygen tubes. 'They didn't want to kill him. Just teach him a lesson. Artemio had become a hero after he'd saved the Mazzettis, after he'd stolen their farm – well, that's how they saw it anyway. Their uncle was making too much of a success of his life and they resented it. The boys were egged on by years of their father's jealousy, but Sauro had no idea of their scheme. I don't even know whether he ever found out.'

'How did Bruna find out?'

'Amabile told her. It almost killed Amabile too. A mother raising murderers, imagine! She heard the boys talking about it and came down to Poggio, all the way through that snow, to see Bruna the next day. She told her herself. One has to admire Amabile's courage. While Artemio's body lay on the bed upstairs, she pleaded that if Bruna took those boys away from her, her whole family would starve. And they would have, too. If you took three men from a family, especially a *pigionale* family, they would not have survived their first winter. Artemio's mother and father knew their grandsons had killed their son, but they still took them and their family in. After that, nobody could face Bruna. They were too ashamed. They deserted her.'

'So my grandmother had to go and live in the house

so recently vacated by her husband's killers?' Nonna asked, clearly feeling some of the hurt that Bruna must have felt one hundred years ago.

Giorgio nodded. 'When Artemio went to have Campo Alto esteemed, the boys were all furious with the *sensale*'s findings. Shortly after the division of goods, Artemio went back up to Campo Alto to start putting the barn in order. He found three truckle beds hidden away and asked the boys why there were beds in the barn. Giuseppe, Pietro and Antonio said that as Campo Alto was closer to Consuma, where they went to drink and have *veglia*, they wanted to carry on sleeping at Campo Alto on their way back home to Omomorto, after their nights out on the town. Artemio told them no way. He said they had to move out and stay out. The boys felt that they had a right to sleep at Campo Alto whenever they wanted to. It all ended in a fight and the boys apparently told him he would pay for his selfishness.'

'Why didn't he just let the boys sleep over?' asked Nonna, trying to make sense of all this new information.

'Because men like Artemio did not believe in young people drinking and dancing. He thought those boys should have been home in their own beds after a hard day's work.'

The room went quiet again, the hum of the refrigerator and Giorgio's laboured breath the only sounds. A palpable feeling of sadness descended upon us. I now felt a deeper grief for Bruna than ever before. Nonna felt it too and put her hand on Giorgio's.

'One thing that I had always been told about the night that Artemio died was that the dogs did not go off,' she said softly. 'In those days dogs were a farmer's alarm system and their silence was one of those strange details that people remembered. Of course they didn't bark, they knew my grandfather's killers. Sauro's boys knew the dogs' names.'

Giorgio pushed his chair back and looked down to fiddle with some gauges on his oxygen tank. 'So, rather than destroy another Bruni family,' he continued, turning his face back to us, 'Bruna let those boys go. If it had been only one – but *three* of Artemio's nephews conspiring to attack their uncle? It broke her heart. She did not want revenge. But she did hold on to the idea of spiritual retribution. Vengeance was for those who had the time to indulge in it. It's important for you to understand that Bruna simply did not have the time to try to enforce a police investigation. That woman, literally, did not have the minutes in the day. She had to provide for her family.'

Nonna agreed and added that Bruna would not have felt worthy of the police attention, either. I thought of how many times Nonna had said that life was cheap in Tuscany. I understood her words now. How insignificant Bruna must have felt before the eyes of the law. She knew her husband's life was unimportant to the authorities.

'What happened to Giuseppe, Pietro and Antonio?' I asked.

'Ho!' Giorgio laughed once, rueful, then sighed and leant forward on the table. 'Over the years Bruna bided her time for news of those boys, and slowly neighbours, friends and relatives brought their fates to her. Giuseppe went to work in France and it was said he had a fight with a Frenchman who stabbed him in the stomach. Pietro developed a tumour in his throat and died like Giuseppe, without ever marrying. Antonio married and had three children. He died of exposure when he went out one night to help a search party find a neighbour's lost child. He became separated from the others and fell into a dam of ice water. They all died before Bruna.

'But,' Giorgio held up his hand, 'don't misunderstand

Bruna. She did not wish horrible deaths upon those boys. Her faith was simple. Her God judged. That was enough for her.'

Nonna shook her head. 'I'd heard about those boys and their deaths, but had no idea they were the ones who killed my grandfather. I've never met Antonio's grandchildren. Lord knows where they are now.'

Giorgio fixed a pointed gaze on Nonna. 'I know where they are. And they do not know anything of their grandfather's sins. You must never let them find out.'

'Yes, that would not be right. It's all too long ago now,' I agreed.

'The reason I've broken Bruna's silence is because it's the right time to do so.' Giorgio's voice, so strong at the beginning of our talk, had turned raspy and tired. His strong Tuscan dialect had begun to slur with the exertion of speaking so much and for so long. His weariness told me it was time to go.

I put my hand over Nonna's, where it still rested over Giorgio's, and thanked him for telling us the truth. He put his other hand on top of mine and, in that direct way he had, stared me in the eye.

'You change the names of the people in your book. Change the names of the farms, too. Everyone knows who everyone is from the farm names. But you tell people what kind of a woman Bruna was. Women like her made Italy what it is today. There were many, many women like Bruna all over Italy. Their spirits live on. You make your readers understand how hard Bruna fought to hold her family together. Remind them of her, for us.'

I said that I would.

Acknowledgements

My greatest thanks must first go to my mother-in-law for her permission to write this book. Nonna and her new husband, Aldo, were always available to answer my never-ending stream of questions. It is their love of the land that is reflected in this book.

My thanks also go to my mother-in-law's sisters, Anita and Maria. Their memories of life under the *mezzadria* system were invaluable. Not to mention the details that they recalled being told of the night their grandfather was murdered. Nonna's eldest sister, Dina, passed away during the writing of this book and I only wish that she could have seen it finally published. It was Dina who was the first of Nonna's sisters to be sent away to work for a rich Florentine family when she was barely eleven years old. We miss her.

I will be forever grateful to farmer extraordinaire Vanni

Cappeletti for his help and patience with my questions as he drove his tractor, cured his prosciutto and milked his sheep for pecorino. Grazie, Vanni.

I am indebted to Franceso Torrini and Angela Bonacorsi for their insights into the lives of the Tuscan farmer. A profound thank-you to you both for the many chats on the terrace of your farm.

A heartfelt thank-you also to Bruna Mencherini and Giancarlo Righini, the Casentino ambulance drivers, both so happy to be available at a moment's notice for queries and puzzle solving.

I so appreciated Tosca Lippi for her wonderful smile, generous interview time and allowing me to share her family's *veglia*.

My special thanks also go to the Communita Montana del Casentino – especially Luca Segantini and Andrea Rossi – for their professionalism and vast knowledge of the *transumanza*, coal makers and the old farming ways.

I owe much to all the following people, without whom this book could not have been written:

Don Guido from the Pratovecchio Church;
Don Francesco Pasetto from the Lonnano Church;
Anna from Pratovecchio Council;
Professor Sesto Vigiani;
Angelo Rossi, the mayor of Pratovecchio;
Karin Stoecker for her unfailing encouragement and mentoring;
Luigi Bonomi for telling me, 'You can do it,' when I needed to hear it;
Tom Gilliatt for his faith in me;
Quirino Baldini, The man from Il Marconi, for his dental knowledge;

Carlo and Carla of Mulin di Bucchio, the old chestnut and flour mill of Stia;

Iolanda Ristori of the Giubbino Alimentare in Pratovecchio;

Don Erasmo at the Consuma Church, Consuma;

Monseigneur Giuseppe Raspini, Casentino social archivist at the Vatican's elderly priest's home in Fiesole;

Luigi Bianchi and Paolo Schiatti of Raggiolo, the chestnut capital of Tuscany;

Emilio Cheveri for his beautiful one-hundred-year old Italian shotgun;

Gemma 'Cici' Conti for her expert editing skills when correcting Italian spelling, and for her help looking after the children when the deadline loomed;

Catie Cellai, Nanette Davis, Janet de Bres and Stephanie Clifford-Smith for reading my early thoughts;

Alison Gilligan for her 'death in a small town' thoughts, and Christine Hogan for her greatly heartening comments;

the Clifford family in Australia, especially my mother and father, June and John, for their belief in this story and me.

And finally, my thanks to my long-suffering children, Natalia and Leo, who never tired of asking, 'Have you finished the book yet, Mum?' And, of course, my deepest thanks to my husband, Paolo. Without him, this book would not have been possible.

Lisa Clifford grew up in Sydney. She moved to Italy when she was sixteen years old and returned to Australia after winning a scholarship to the Australian Film, Television and Radio School. Following a career in journalism that included reporting for 2GB, Mix FM and Channel Ten news, Lisa was associate producer of the Channel Ten late news. Throughout her career, she continued to travel to Italy, corresponding for 2UE, the ABC's Radio National and the Voice of America News Service. She is the author of *Walking Sydney* and *The Promise – an Italian Romance*. Lisa now lives in Florence with her husband and two children.